NORTH-EAST

DIALECT:

SURVEY AND

WORD-LIST

Bill Griffiths

Published in Great Britain by
The Centre for Northern Studies
Department of Historical & Critical Studies
University of Northumbria
Newcastle upon Tyne
NE1 8ST

Printed by Athenaeum Press Ltd.
Dukes Way
Team Valley
Gateshead
NE11 0PZ

ISBN 0 9511472 4 2

CONTENTS

1. A Survey of Dialect in the North-East

Page 5

2. Guide to the Development of Northern Pronunciation

Page 48

3. Word List

Page 57

4. General Bibliography

Page 140

3

For Gordon Patrickson of Seaham
For his encouragement at the start.

A Survey of Dialect in the North-East

A dialect is a local standard of speech, not necessarily a written standard, indeed often seen as contrasting with the 'superior' speech and spelling conventions of a centralised / authorised 'norm'. (The prefix dia- ought to indicate separateness, not subordination as such.) Dialect as lower in status is a result of the promotion of 'Queen's English' over at least the last 120 years, affecting both spoken and written propriety; but the demotion of dialect in the North may feasibly date back to the decline in status in Scots after the Union of Scotland and England in 1603; while the rise of the London standard was undoubtedly assisted by the introduction of printing in this country from 1476 on. Dictionaries from the late 17th century on similarly contributed to that durable written standard - modern 'English' - which has so influenced all the spoken Englishes in turn.

Back in Anglo-Saxon times, the political and social importance of language was already recognised: what else after was the nation (þēod) but its language? King Alfred, in personally encouraging the translation of major Latin texts into Old English (the vernacular of the day) surely appreciated the role of language in maintaining West Saxon and English identity against the Viking insurgents. In the mid 10th century, when the monastic system was more fully developed, Late West Saxon was selected as the norm for written communication (history, laws, sermons, writs, letters etc), and the business of the monasteries themselves. This encouraged a consistency of vocabulary and spelling. The collapse of the native dynasty at the arrival of William the Conqueror, and the end of that long tradition of patronage that provided the unity and power to ensure scribal conformity round the country, not only meant the elimination of this first attempt to provide a 'standard English': it left an already challenged language in a condition of flux, unregulated and unsupported by an alien ruling class, and about to fragment into regional dialects, where change would take place at unequal rates. Spoken English was to occupy a low status, in contrast to the Norman-French used at Court and the Latin of official records, and this did not change until the 14th century.

A Northern text of that time explains the need for literature in English thus:

And bathe klerk and laued man
English understand kan,
That was born in Ingeland,
And lang haves ben thar in wonand,
Bot al men can noht, I-wis,
Understand Latin and Frankis.

(For both cleric and lay man can understand English, if he was born in England and has been living there for a long time; but all men cannot, I reckon, understand Latin and French.)

Curiously it was not the influential South but the Midlands and the North that pioneered many of the features basic to modern English e.g. forms of the verb in -s̲ like 'he says', 'she has', 'he casts', as opposed to Southern 'he saith', 'she hath', 'he casteth' etc., forms preserved in the King James Bible out of respect for earlier Southern translators of the text. Movements of population from the East Midlands and the North into London by the 15th century seem to have ensured the official language of the capital became the highly modified North-based variety, not the more decorative (and more conservative) Chaucerian type. At the same time, word order became simplified and standardised; for Middle English included a new syntax based on time and causation, that remodelled the jigsaw-like concept of words fitting together and produced a much smoother, more expressive (linear) process.

The beginning of the transformation of Old English can be traced to the North of the country in the 9th-10th centuries, when the highly inflected system of Old English (somewhat like modern German, with genders and cases of nouns whose endings changed with their role in the sentence, and a complex verb system) started to shift towards the easier-to-use ('analytic') grammar of modern English, with verbals or phrase-like verbs and prepositions ('to', 'at', 'of', 'for' etc.) doing the work of case endings, while the sentence itself became moulded on the sense order of words (subject-verb-object) something we now take for granted as the English language's greatest asset.

The already sometimes confusing case endings of Old English (with minimal distinction between subject and object for example) would have helped prompt this move to reform. Also the accent or emphasis in Old English on the root (often the first) syllable of a word meant that the final weak syllable that carried the inflexional information tended to be obscured or entirely dropped. With the lack of effective means of maintaining Old English as it was, and the increasing pressures for compromise with Old Norse and Old French speakers in the country, it is little surprise that English entered a phase of change and development, with different forms of Middle English emerging in different regions.

The process by which Old Norse came to affect Old English is detailed by Dieter Kastovsky (1992). With Viking settlement continuing into the 10th century and even 11th century kings of England drawn from Viking descent, it may be assumed that the earliest settlers from Scandinavia saw little need to modify their language: they would have remained Old Norse speakers, or perhaps have become bilingual. After the mid 11th century however, the status of Old Norse radically diminished, in line with the loss of political status for the Scandinavian element in England, until Old Norse was but another 'normal minority language'. By about 1200 it is likely the Old Norse was largely abandoned as a spoken language in England, and as the Viking-stock settlers moved into conformity with the local form of English, they brought with them an impressive number of loan-words from their original language. The paradox is that there were a limited number of loan-words from Old Norse while Viking political power was in the ascendant (800-1050 AD), and chose not to mix, but a large number of common everyday words were transfered from Old Norse into Middle English in the 13th century, to become part of standard London English in the 15th century e.g 'sky, 'egg', 'they'.

As Vikings only settled in the Northern half of the country, the Midlands, East Anglia and North to the lowlands of Scotland, it is here their vocabulary might be expected to have the greatest impact and to have become a distinctive feature of the local 'dialect' from the Middle English period onward. More Norse-based words than made it into 'standard English' are found in the Northern dialects, e.g. taum 'fishing-line', cree 'animal pen', marra 'workmate'. In fact, the history of Northern dialect in the last 400 years or so seems might be measured in terms of the

8

gradual loss of this non-standard vocabulary, in the face of the increasing status of 'modern English', that originally Northern idea, now reimported from the South.

The loss of distinctive vocabulary (including Old English words e.g. wark 'to ache' as well as French e.g aran-web 'spider-web' and Old Norse examples) is not consistent, giving the impression that words must always have had a limited local use. This is probably deceptive. Although rural areas still yield more Norse-based terms than industrial ones (e.g. Ellis (1985) on Pennines and central Cumbria), strictly speaking this is indicative of an area in which a set of word preferences (possibly regional rather than local), made at one historic point, has resisted change (irrespective of population modification or continuity thereafter). For Norse-based words were surely available throughout the North in the Middle English period, and though never codified as such it is not inappropriate to think in terms of a Common Northern pool of vocabulary. (The high status of Scotland and Scottish language in the 15-16th centuries might have been significant here.) I am not convinced by the arguments of those who maintain that Northumberland dialect is relatively free of Norse-based words because few Vikings settled there. The good people of Northumberland speak, like everyone else in the North, a compromise between 'standard English' and some common traditional Northern form of English, in a combination that emerged locally over hundreds of years, with little regard to race or parentage.

Let us explore the same argument in relation to County Durham. Little sign of any largescale Viking settlement here. Few or no place-names in Danish thorpe/by or Norwegian thwaite, and finds of 'hogback' stone coffins (considered typical of Viking culture) limited to examples along the River Tees. Yet in Easington District, in the East of the County, along the coast, there are Norse-based words used in place-names alongside Old English-based terms, with no Viking population to account for their presence. In general, such evidence is discarded on the basis that County Durham suffered such upheavals of population in the Industrial Revolution that its dialect is no safe indicator of early usage. But the first Ordnance Survey maps from the middle of the 19th century were made before the East of the County became a major coal-producing area and would surely have been checked with local landowners whose memory went back into the early 19th century, and with local deeds. This evidence could therefore be of considerable importance.

It is to be noted that the 1840s Ordnance Survey uses dene (OE) for major valleys near the coast but gill (ON) for a minor or side valley, burn (OE) for the major stream within a dene, but beck (ON) for a minor watercourse. Here the two words have existed side-by-side in a pre-industrial context, with mutually adapted roles. Snook (ON) and ness (OE) similarly both occur in coastal names, with less certain distinction. But in case it be suggested that this results from a tidying-up by the makers of maps at the Ordnance Survey (evidence on how the names of English features were first recorded was lost in the bombing of World War 2), we can add evidence from wills and maps preceding the C19th. Thus a 1774 map of field-names round Old Seaham in East Durham includes probable Viking elements in 'High Holms' and 'Low Holms', 'Howfoot', 'High Garth', 'Mid Garth' and 'Low Garth', 'North Muzlicarrs' and 'West Muzlicarrs' and, notably, a field called 'Eleven

Score Rigs' in which __Rigs__ is altered to the more standard (non-Viking) __Ridgs__ ('ridges') as an afterthought.

To add to the complexity of the situation, it is by no means always easy to distinguish a word that is purely of Old Norse (Viking) origin. Some words that passed into Middle English (Common North) were common to Northern OE (Anglian) and ON e.g. __gang__ (to go), __bairn__ (a child), and so became markers of Northern English in contrast with Southern (esp. West Saxon) usage. Old Norse also influenced the alternative pronunciations g/y, k/ch, sk/sh in favour of the former, sometimes leading to doublets e.g. __gate__ and __yat__, __carl__ and __churl__, __scoot__ and __shoot__. These may exist side-by-side, modifying in meaning. Thus in the County as whole, two types of 'gate' are found, one from OE __yæt__, one from ON __gatt__, developing distinctive meanings of 'pasture right' and 'road, way' respectively. In short, words from different origins do not have strict local boundaries, but often occur together, and have survived side by side with mutually adapted roles.

Tracing the origin of words remains a major puzzle. Forms in k-, g- or sk- may sometimes be native forms influenced by ON pronunciations, as is surely the case with __kirk__ for 'church'. It is not always easy, therefore, to determine between an authentic Old Norse borrowing and an Old English term influenced by Old Norse. Tracing an etymological source may help; so may the evidence of later distribution: words that generally limited to the North, the East Midlands and/or East Anglia (all areas of Viking settlement) may be accorded a Norse origin e.g. __big__ (barley), __chare__, __dill__, __garth__, __gome__, __hap__, __kist__, __kittle__, __lowe__, __lowp__, __lug__, __sike__, __steg__; those with a wider currency (e.g. also found in the West

11

Midlands and the South) like <u>dunch</u>, <u>howk</u>, <u>nesh</u>, <u>poke</u>, <u>sharn</u>, <u>snead</u>, <u>sweal</u>, may be Southern in origin or amalagams of Southern and Northern terms.

The difficulty often is that the word record is very incomplete. A word with Southern affinities may still have had lost or unrecorded forms in Scandinavian tongues that only emerge in Modern Icelandic or Swedish, say. This could indicate there was indeed a similar word in Old Norse, though no record of it survives in an Anglo-Viking context. The problem persists: a word recorded both in dialect and Modern Dutch may go back to a valid early Anglo-Frisian term, or could be a medieval or modern borrowing from Dutch, e.g. during the 15th-17th centuries, when shipping in the North Sea (and in some measure international trade) was dominated by the Netherlands.

One useful reference point ought to be the 'Metrical Life of Cuthbert', a poetic text from Co.Durham datable to ca.1450, since literature was presumably written to be read aloud and should not be dominated by traditional legal formulas as formal documents are prone to be. But the text proves to combine some recognisable dialect forms with others that are Southern or standard but omits (or is ignorant of or fails to use) a number of what now are everyday modern dialect favourites. The following examples from the language of the poem illustrate the continuity from Old English or Old Norse through Middle English (Northern) to present-day dialect:

ay (ever, source of <u>aye</u>=yes), **barne** (<u>bairn</u> - child), **bigg** (to build), **cleke** (<u>click</u> - to catch), **deand** (<u>dee-in'</u> - doing), **dyng** (<u>ding</u> - to beat), **fande** (found), **flaide** (scared), **garte** (<u>garr'd</u> - compelled), **gere** (<u>gear</u> -

equipment), **getyn** (getten - got), **graith** (to ready), **grett** (cried), **hedewark** (headache), **kest...up** (cast... up, but not hoy or throw), **kist** (chest), **lapped** (folded, wrapped), **lasse** (lass), **laykes** (games), **low** (lowe - flame), **nesche** (nesh - soft), **nevys** (neeves - fists), **noke** (nook), **ryve** (rive - to tear), **slockyn** (sloken - to quench), **sper** (speer - to enquire), **stour** (commotion), **tane** (tiun - taken), **telled** (told), **tome** (tium - empty), **wyfe** (wife - woman); plus the Northern Middle English (but now more Scots-sounding) **kende** (kenn'd - knew), **kirk** (church) and **sark** (shirt).

The tendency to separation between England and France, politically, in the 13th century, and the need for some basis of unity in the face of the disasters and upheavals of the 14th century, encouraged the rise in status of English. But it was an already much modified and distant relative of the Common Northern speech via Midlands filters, that filled the gap and became the approved standard of the London region. This soon comes to have an effect, for written records were the product of specially educated clerks, for whom some measure of standardisation of language and spelling was likely to be taken as proof of qualification.[1] There is thus disappointingly little dialectal evidence to be gleaned from:

1. *Records of Newcastle Guilds* in *Records of Early English Drama* ed. J.J. Anderson (Toronto 1982), where (with dates occurring): **kirk** (1508), **yatt** (gate,

---

[1] *A Linguistic Atlas of Late Medieval England* (ed. Angus McIntosh et al., 4 vols, Aberdeen 1986) includes in vol.III (pp.92-7) a comprehensive list of medieval deeds originating in Co. Durham, such as wills, letters, etc, with details of dialect forms, at Vol.III pp.92-97.

1503), **ledder** (leather, 1590), **ffouel** (fool, 1616), **heaid** (head, 1628), **wishing** (washing, 1624).

2. *The Grassmen's Accounts of St Giles at Durham* (Surtees Society vol.95) where for 1632: **loone** (lane), **yet** (gate), **dicke** (ditch); for 1734: **watter** (water), **leazes** (pasture).

3. *Jacob Bee's Diary* (Surtees Society vol.118, 1910, pp.45-63, covering 1681-1706):
betwixt (between), **murthur** (murder), **bishel** (bushel), **streen'd** (strained), **moneth** (month).

Forms like yet, leazes, moneth, seem to indicate continuity from Old English, but occur alongside Viking-influenced forms e.g. kirk, dicke; all these local forms are relatively rare examples, however, within a framework of recognisable standard English text. It would seem that the Common Northern English language I posit was being actively rejected, not surprisingly after the removal of the Scots seat of monarchy and patronage to London in the early 17th century and the military threat from the Highland clans in the 18th century.

After K.M.Petyt (*The Study of Dialect* (London, 1980, p.69) we must assume that within the educated or governing class the spread of standard English (especially as a standard vocabulary, with local variations of pronunciation) must have been fairly well established by about 1700, at least in towns, for otherwise the point of Edward Chicken's joke in his poem about unintelligible (or rather, comically untypical) pitmen would have been a pointless one. Edward Chicken lived from 1698 to 1746 in Newcastle, and his work, *The Collier's Wedding; A Poem*, written in 1720, entered print in 1764. It is in fluent rhyming standard English

14

couplets, except for bits of direct popular (especially male) speech, for which the appropriate dialect is used. But the speakers are the strange, uncouth, uninhibited miners beginning to settle in Benwell, and the point of his bawdy good-natured satire would be entirely lost if there were no difference between the way they spoke and the way the (better) citizens of Newcastle conceived English ought to be spoken.

As it has been possible to reprint the whole text (1985), I will summarise its dialect content here rather than give excerpts. Chicken's standardised spelling largely ignores the diphthongs (two vowels slurred into one) which would have taken the place of pure long vowels by the end of the Middle Ages. But in lexical terms there are many words he seems to be indicating as non-standard for his day: fash and dame are clearly French in origin; the occasional term (e.g. tew) may be a survival of Old English; and yet others (rive 'rip', cod 'pillow') indicate Norse influence. This combination seems to have already been typical of Northern speech, and the source in this case must surely have been a country (i.e. non-urban) dialect, but whether of Northumberland or the Pennines is less certain. Heslop (1892-6, p.xvi) posits a move to the city from the higher inland regions: "To these dalesmen [i.e. from Tynedale and Riddesdale] we owe the strong clanship of the colonies of pitmen and keelmen scattered along Tyneside and throughout the colliery districts."

The growth of mining in the 18th century (arguably from the late C16th) must have brought together into the vicinity of Newcastle many workers from outlying areas whose speech clearly was not the modified semi-standard spoken English of town and certainly nothing like the pure written standard English of the educated townsfolk. Chicken himself was a staunch Tory (the party of land, and the Church of England, with an inclination to the Stuart succession); here he was satirizing the country-based speech of the new industrial sub-class (industrial development being pioneered by the Whigs, hence 'Geordie', the talk of the workers on the side of the Hanoverian dynasty). These incoming workers retained the full range of North-Eastern vocabulary probably from a number of areas, with many more non-standard words than were admitted into polite North-Eastern speech and the implication of Chicken's poem is that their arrival was something of a shock and a cause of wonder. Ridiculous or snobbish on the face of it, but clearly the new industrial class's language, like their behaviour, was something not easily acceptable to those who regarded themselves as the guardians of true English.

Of course, if there were justice, the satire and astonishment would have been the other way round, for the Geordies were true to the tradition of English in the whole area much more than those who practised 'correct' English, and in fact the sheer weight of numbers of the new industrial class soon restored a measure of respect for their speech. In the 1790s, Geordie came to the cultural forefront with the new emphasis on republicanism and democracy, which nationalism and anti-Napoleonism was unable to quench. It was a language that already approached the standard in terms of grammar, but was significantly independent in vocabulary and pronunciation. This regionalism does not seem to have been exploited by later Chartists or Trade Unionists, who used printed notices in standard English, doubtless as an indication of the national level of their aspirations, so that as the 19th century progresses, the local dialectal, cultural or political initiative seems to wane. Regionalism returned to favour in the later C19th with the creation of County Councils and official recognition or exploitation of local identities, and dialect earned serious study at an academic level at last, as witness the great *Dialect Dictionary* project of the English Dialect Society which was completed by about 1900 by Joseph Wright. But in everyday terms, dialect was sometimes accorded a rather patronising role: not uncommonly Geordie speech became the standard of the commercial music-hall, a source of entertainment and fun (sometimes at Geordie's own expense), reflecting, it may seem, the exhaustion of the authentic democratic initiative and the increasing preference of workers to identify themselves with the 'progressive' Victorian state. (Thus Jack Lawson says, with apparent pride, of his well-travelled father: "he told wonderful stories in choice English never using a word of dialect." *A Man's Life*, 1932, ch.2) Socialism has played a very ambiguous role: its international aspect might seem to argue against petty local differentials, and yet the large organised workforces of the 20th century and the typical heavy industries like coal, iron and ship-building have proved useful (if incidental) contexts for dialect continuity. In turn, dialect provided the workforce with identity and cohesion, and more practically with a technical vocabulary on which effective and safe work pratices could be built. For industry and the industrial dialect was spreading south, with ship-building to Sunderland, and with mining to first the north and west and then the rest of County Durham during the 19th century, merging with local speech to form the various grades of pitmatic still recognisable today.

And these two great industries are worth considering for what evidence they may give of the sources of Geordie: 'rustic' may be the first impression,[2] but mining and maritime vocabularies surely played a part in shaping and distinguishing this new proletarian speech. A surprisingly high number of seemingly Dutch-derived words are recorded in Geordie: **blare, canty, clavers, corve, crack, cranky, dwamy, har, hunker, keek, kite, shool, skipper, stithe, yammer** - for example. Here too we may add **Pea-jacket** (see Barbara Strang *A History of English*, London, 1970, p.75), and **plack**, which seems derived from the name of a C15th Flemish coin. Other words, apparently Dutch-based, may have come in through maritime contact, though relevant to a more general context: **cant, elsin, geck, gliff, haar, hoy, kit, knack, mafted, mizzle, plote, pluff, pubble, scudder, yuke.** Distribution may be a helpful guide here: potentially Dutch-based words that are or were current in seaboard counties e.g. **cavil, hoy, har,** have a good chance of being modern additions from maritime contact, and it is apossibility at least worth considering that it was Dutch influence through the coastal trade that first set Geordie slightly apart from

---

[2] The verb put is used alike of propelling a keel-boat as of a coal-tub, as it had earlier been of a bull pushing with its horns. So too gove/goaf is transfered from the section of an agricultural wooden building to the span between props in a mine. 'Kevilling', the alloting of work-stations in a mine, is apparently based on agricultural practice too. "The most common method of working the meadows was to divide them into strips or dales, and these were allocated annually by lot or rotation, or on a more permanent basis." p.134, A.R.H. Baker & R.A.Butlin *Studies of Field Systems* (London, 1973).

the rustic speech of Northumberland or Durham, a separateness soon to be reinforced by miners: for with coal being shipped by water and workers of all trades meeting recreationally in Newcastle this connection between the two needs little explanation.

If we look at the sort of terms connected with mining (not mentioned by Chicken, who is looking only at the private life of his characters), some apparent bias in the vocabulary emerges. This time a major factor would seem to be Old Norse from which the following are believed to come: **at bank, bowk, bleck, goaf, kirve, kist, marra, skeets, skep, skip,** and **swalley**. Others uncertain of source, but quite possibly also from Norse, are: **bait, buntins, canches, dreg, hoggers, hough, kevel** (mallet), **nick, put, sprag, stour** and **toom**. A few may evidence connection with Dutch (**cavel, corve, hunkers, stithe**), or French (**chauldron, rammel**). Where could this extra element have come from? Copper-mining was encouraged in Cumberland by Queen Elizabeth's minister Cecil in 1566, and coal-mining important in the Newcastle area by the 16th century; while lead-mining was put on a commercial basis in the Pennines in the late 17th century. Some use may have been made of German expertise (whence the word <u>kibble</u>?). The Pennine/ Cumberland conection may be sufficient to account for an apparent Viking bias in this mining terminology, but it may be unhelpful to stress to such pedigrees in this context. After all, the mix is not untypical of the emerging Tyneside speech: more conservative than urban/London English, but dynamic, inventive, ecclectic, and serving practically an increasing industrial population.

Mike Shields (*Lore & Language* 10) makes an informed attempt to distinguish between sub-types of Geordie (strictly the speech of Newcastle, he says, but could be extended to the area up to 5 miles north and south of the Lower Tyne, p.6). In general, he sees Geordie (Tyneside, here represented by T) as closer to the accent of Northumberland than of Co.Durham (D) though Sunderland is included in his wider Geordie area. This speech is typified by a tendency to pure vowels rather than diphthongs e.g. T {fe:s} than D {'fejus} ('face'), T {rod} than D {ro-ud} ('road'), indicating later smoothing in the urban vowels. Some vocabulary contrasts are as follows: T **divnt** than D **dinnut** (Shields/Sunderland **dee-unt** i.e. don't); T **bullet** ('sweet') than D **ket**. **Aa'z** he sees as an older form than **Aa'm** - correctly, and an interesting sign that even Geordie itself has been changing and receiving input from standard English: this particular change can be dated to the late 19th century. Mid-Tyne he notes as being more conventional than true Geordie e.g. **don't** than **divn't**, **you** than **yi**, **yes** than **aye**. "I believe this modification may perhaps be due to extensive Irish immigration to this area." (p.6).

He lists the following as typical Geordie words:

bairn (child), **boody** (earthenware), **bullet** (sweet), **clag** (to stick), **clarts** (mud), **dee** (do), **deek** (look at! see! [but Romany by origin]), **dunch** (crash into), **fadge** (flat-loaves), **femmer** (frail), **galluses** (braces), **gan** (go), **glow** (window [a misunderstanding of lowe?]), **gob** (mouth), **gwaak** (stare foolishly, gawk), **haad** (hold), **howway** (come on), **hoy** (throw), **lad**, **lass**; **lowp** (jump, leap), **marrer** (mate), **poss** (wash in hot water), **shuggy-boat** (fairground swing), **stot** (bounce), **stotty-cake** (flat loaves, oven-bottom bread) and of course, **canny**, which can be used of health, people, children, animals, places, numbers etc., and also as an adverb ("gan canny").

Most of these would be intelligible anywhere in the North-East; some, arguably, always had a wider curency than Tyneside alone, while others will have spread into Durham usage form the high status of Geordie speech in the 19th century.

For example of the Norse-based (and so pre-industrial) elements in Mike Shields' list (**clag**, **femmer**, **lowp**, **marrer**), none of these is mentioned by Kennet as in use in Durham ca.1700; only **clag** occurs in Durham in Bailey (1810). All are known to Brockett (collecting words in Newcastle in 1846). Many come into use in Co.Durham by the end of the 19th century as recorded by Palgrave, and there can be little doubt the dialect peculiarities spread south with the industry it served.

Can we get through such a premised over-layer back to a recognisable pre-industrial Durham dialect, in pronunciation or vocabulary? To reach something definitively 'Durham', we would need to return to the agricultural speech of the County, and this is not as easy as it seems, for early records are scarce. But from the 17th century onwards there does emerge an interest in the study of language for its own sake, which provides some evidence of local usage. The first such study I have come across relevant to dialect in the 'modern' period is Alexander Gil's *Logonomia Anglica* (2nd edn, London 1621). This is a short general account, in Latin, of various features of the English language, like spelling and grammar; but on pages 16-17 there is a summary of Northern Dialect, with examples of pronunciation (e.g. "beað pro both") and vocabulary (e.g. "sark pro shirt"), but the author is referring to practices "Apud

21

meos...Lincolniensis" ('among my native folk in Lincolnshire'), and this is therefore not exact evidence for further North.

For the North-East, recognition began with the publication of a small number of Yorkshire dialect texts at this time e.g. George Meriton's *A Yorkshire Dialogue* (1683). Perhaps these reflected the growing status and awareness of Yorkshire gentry in the 17th century. (See Musgrove, pp.224-5, 247.) If so, they represent in some measure a rejection of the London standard and an assertion of regional integrity. Or they may have been responses to new theories about language like that ennunciated by Thomas Sprat, Secretary of the Royal Society, in 1667, who recommended "a close, naked, natural way of speaking - positive expressions, clear sense, a native easiness, bringing all things as near the mathematical plainness as they can, and prefering the language of artisans, countrymen, and merchants before wits and scholars."[3] Of these early pioneers, Meriton lived 1634-1711, in Northallerton, and printed not only short dialect texts (which might have appealed to a purely local audience) but added his own glossary, implying that he was aware of outside scholastic interest. From this glossary the following items are selected for their relevance to the North-East (I abbreviate or paraphrase his explanations):

arfe (afraid), **awd** (old), **beestling** (rich milk), **cawd** (cold), **clim** (climb), **crawe/creake** (crow), **deau** (do), **deaun** (done), **dee** (die), **dike** (pond), **ding** (hit), **don** (to put on), **dree** (to endure), **een** (eyes), **feaul** (fool), **flee** (to fly), **fra** (from), **geay/gang** (go), **git** (get), **gitten**

---

[3] qu. Eric Mottram 'Poetry and mathematics: an introduction' *Reality Studios* 2/3 (1980) 39-44 p.43

(got), **greet** (weep), **haud/hawd** (hold), **haver** (oats), **hing** (hang), **ive our stable** (in our stable), **Ise** (I am), **keauks** (cooks), **kend** (known), **kites** (bellies), **kittle** (tickle), **knawe** (know), **kye** (cows), **lang** (long), **leauke** (look), **leet** (to alight), **ligg** (to lie), **lows** (to loosen), **macks** (makes), **mawks** (maggots), **mell** (meddle), **mickle** (much), **monny** (many), **mun** (must), **neane** (no one), **newke** (nook), **neem** (eam, uncle), **nut** (not), **onny** (any), **ore** (over), **owght** (aught), **owse** (ox), **pokes** (sacks, bags), **put** (to butt, push with the horns), **rame** (to roam), **reek** (to smoke), **rencky** (large and well-made), **rive** (to tear), **rowt** (to bellow), **sall** (shall), **sarke** (shirt), **seeay** (so), **selld** (sold), **sike** (such), **sine** (since), **slocken** (to quench [thirst]), **snawke** (inhale), **sneck** (latch), **snithe** (cold, piercing), **snurles** (nostrils), **speer** (find out by enquiring), **stee** (ladder), **stob** (thorn), **tack** (take), **tawk** (talk), **telld** (told), **tite** (neat, tidy), **tweay** (two), **wad** (would), **wark** (work, fuss), **warse** (worse), **weaud** (wod, mad), **weel** (well), **weese** (we are, we will), **wheay** (who), **wheesht!** (hush!), **whope** (to hope), **yawd** (horse), **yeaud** (to go).

Here is a mix of non-standard pronunciations e.g. dee for 'die', points of grammar e.g. telled for 'told' (the Yorkshire form is closer to Old English than the Mordern English form is) - and of non-standard vocabulary. Many of the unfamiliar items here have their origin in Old Norse (Viking), being words adopted into Northern English that never made it into 'standard' i.e. Southern English; other words are common to Old English and Old Norse; and a few may be authentic survivals from Old English that were abandoned in Southern speech e.g. speer, yeaud.

Another figure from the Royal Society who took an interest in local dialect was John Ray, naturalist and linguist. Slightly earlier than Meriton, John Ray had published his *Collection of English Words, Not Generally Used...* (London, 1674), whose first edition included a considerable number of words attested elsewhere to be in use in Durham e.g. **addle, amell, anauntrins, anent, arles, asker, astite** etc. (these are included in my glossary, so I do not list in full here). The third edition of 1737 was enlarged by information from Francis Brokesby, rector of Rowley in East Yorkshire, and other informants from e.g. Cumberland, and includes a much larger range of words I believe to be relevant to the North-East though he did not seem to be using any specific source of information in that area, and does not distinguish any word as in use in Co.Durham.

Many of these additional terms are also found in Bishop Kennet's 'Etymological Collections of English Words and Provincial Expressions', a manuscript dictionary surviving as British Library MS Lansdowne 1033 (vol. 99 of Bishop Kennet's Collection). White Kennet, 1660-1728, Vicar of Amersden, Oxfordshire, between 1685 and 1700, and later Bishop of Peterborough, constructed this word list from ca.1690 onwards, using printed sources and correspondence with e.g. George Hickes (the Anglo-Saxonist, and for a period Kennet's friend and tutor, though later disassociating himself from Kennet's Whig politics). Kennet's list appears to depend mainly on printed sources, while Ray seems to have been doing original research, so that terms common to both lists (often with identically worded definitions) ought to originate in Ray; but Ray gives no specific location for the currency of any of the words he prints, whereas Kennet does attribute a number of these words, common to both their lists, to Durham. It is likely therefore that they shared access to some local word-list, or local contact; but

24

who that ultimate source was remains unknown, whether (even) visiting antiquarian or resident of the county.[4]

Although I use Kennet's list in my Glossary, as this is the first 'modern' word list specifying items for County Durham, I excerpt below all those terms I have traced in his manuscript bearing an attribution to Durham i.e. labelled 'Dunelm'.

barrow in Dunelm. a grove
brew [ale]wife
cawel a basket in the North; hence a Cawel is a chicken-coop [in Durham]
daw to be able "I did as I dught"
dene a valley
eard the earth or ground
earfe fearfull, timerous
eath, easie [Northern]... Dunelm. eathy.
eld-father grandfather...eld-mother
to fea or fow to cleanse or empty, as to fea a Pond, a Privy etc.
gimmers door-hinges. Dunelm. & jimmers esp. of a pair of doors
a gimmer tree a tree that grows double from the root
to grath(e) a hous or room, to deck it or dress it up neat and fine
har small rain...it harrs it rains in small drops
haws, hause, hose throat [Northern] [from] Sax. hals, collum, which is therefore still halse. Dunelm.

---

[4] Correspondants I have been able to locate are Wm Claxton of Winyard who supplied Stowe and Camden with local material; and, after the Civil War, James Mickleton, Barrister, 1637-1693, who collected local documents for J. Davies, compiler of *The Ancient Rites & Monuments of the Monastical & Cathedral Church of Durham* (London, 1672).

a heckle a corslet or any covering, as the heckle of a fighting cock. Dunelm. Sax. hæcile, hæcla, hecele...hence the skin or outside of an ox is call'd his hachle or hackle. Dunelm. a rough-hackled or smooth-hackled Ox

hefled w**ted, as in a heffled manner. Dunelm. Sax. hæfed [Lat.] habilus [but Wright (Dialect Dictionary): haffle/heffle - to stammer, falter, prevaricate]

a hemble or hemle a hovel or house [Yorx]. And in Dunelm. any place covered over head and open on both sides is call'd a hemle or hemble. Sax. hælme

huly peevish, fretfull. When a man is not easily plaes'd or seems captious and forward, then is said to be 'huly', and a 'huly man'

the lafe [Durham] or lave [Yorx] the residue or all that is left.

to latch to light, to fall, as a Cat latchath upon her feet.

a leak or leche a gutter

Leath-wake... flexible [re] Cuthbert's body [with ref. to Davies, *Rites & Monuments of the Monastery Church of Durham* p.105]... a Lith-wake Man, a clever nimble fellow [?confusion of lithe and lych/lyke i.e. OE lic 'body']

a loom or lumm a chimney. Dunelm. from Sax. leoma, jubur

lough a pond or standing pool

maug, meaugh a wive's brother [Durham], maugh [Yorx]

midden a maxen or dunghill in the North... midding [Durham/Westmoreland]

to ming to mind or observe... minging a mentioning or putting in mind

neaf the fist [Northern]... a neaf or naife, a hand or fist [Durham]... neif hand or fist [Durham/Westmoreland]...neaves fists [Yorx]

26

nesh soft, tender [Durham]. Flabby, as a nesh man, nesh grass.

to note to eat...Islandica [in Icelandic] At Niota...[Latin] comedere

oky, ouky, ooky, woky, wooky moist, sappy [Durham]...weaky moist [Northern]

ome the smoak, reek, stith or vapour of hot liquids is call'd ome... as the ome of salt pans

oxter, oxterns [Northern] an armpit, the armpits. Oxtar, Oxtars [Durham]

paddock a young frog

to punne to pound or beat in a mortar

racen, a racken or racen pot-hangers in Yorkshire; in the bishoprick of Durham a racen-crouk

to rame to weep or cry [Durham]; to reem [Lancs.]

ream cream [Northern, Durham, Yorx, Westmoreland]

rip to rob or spoil

roomy wide, spacious, with room enough

to rowl or rowt to roar

to ryple to lie, to romance

to slant to mock or lie or dissemble

a snædd a sithe snædd, the handle of a sithe [scythe]

snaw snow

snedder slim, slender... snether or snedder... a snether woman.

snell sharp, cold, as a 'snell wind', a sharp piercing wind, 'a snell morning', a bitter cold morning

snod, snog smoothe, sleek... as He is snodly gear'd or snogly gear'd... wheat ears are said to be 'snod' when they have no beards or awms

a spa*e of water a little standing pool of water

a spink of fire a spark [Durham]...a whink of fire a spark [Westmoreland], a spink [Durham]

a sprete a pole, a long staff

swere dull, heavy, as, a swere fellow

to toom wool to card it

werke to ake or pain. As, my head werkes, my teeth
werke
whilk somebody, a certain person
to wunn to dwell or reside... to woon... where woon
you? i.e. where dwell you?
yary sharp, ready. a yary fellow [Kent], yare
[Durham] Sax. gearwe
yewk the [itc]h [Durham]... to yuck to itch, to have
an itching in the skin [Northern]

This list is notable in several respects. Firstly, it
contains a high proportion of words derivable from
Old English, though whether selection plays a role
here, or whether the informant perhaps sought
words from a traditional (rural/domestic) context, or
even words relevant to an OE etymology, is unclear.
Secondly, it includes a moderate number of Norse-
derived words (**fea**, **grath**, **maug**, **neaf**, **note**,
paddock, **rame**, **rowt**, **snell**); and it seems unlikely
he has excluded others, for Kennet was interested in
words from all sources (as with his Icelandic
parallel for note). The implication here is that
Norse-based words were already part of the pre-
industrial Durham dialect. And thirdly,
surprisingly few of the words above are in use in
present day Durham, or have been recorded in use
this century. This suggests very considerable shifts
of vocabulary came about with the industrialisation
of the area.

At the end of the 'agricultural' epoch, a further word
list was made, as printed in the glossary to John
Bailey's *General View of the Agriculture of the
Country of Durham* (1810). This book shows
considerable local detailed knowledge, and is
unlikely to be based on previous work (e.g. shows
little accord with Ray); there is therefore no reason
to doubt that it presents a valid (if gentlemanly and

28

occasionally learned) summary of vocabulary in the County (or some part of the County) at the time, with a necessary bias towards terms of agricultural significance (likely anyway to be conservative/ traditional). I re-type the glossary from the 1810 edition direct. However, there exists a reprint of the glossary as a modern booklet (in Durham University Library, Palace Green), which contains some explanatory material and a few entries not in the original. I place this matter in curly brackets {}, for the extra entries may have come from some valid second printing or edition of the book, rather than being modern/editorial. (An original note on p.374 relates to pronunciation: "A...is [often] sounded like yaw: as yal, ale; and where so sounded is marked ā)

adlings - earnings
amel - between
arder - fallow quarter {ploughed land left fallow}
arles or earles - earnest money
arnut - earth nut
bain - ready, near
{**balk** - ridge between two furrows}
batts - islands in rivers, or flat grounds adjoining them
beck - a brook or rivulet
berrier - a thresher
bink - a seat of stones, wood, or sods, made mostly against the front of a house
blash - to plash [sic]
bleb - a drop
brake - a large harrow
braugham - a collar which goes round a horse's neck to draw by. {braffen}
brent - steep
brissel - to scorch or dry very hard with fire
bumble-kites - bramble berries (fruit of *Rubus fructicosus*)

burn - a rivulet
buse - a stall; as cow buse, hay buse
buste - a mark set upon sheep with tar, &c.
bute or boot - money given in bartering horses, &c.
to equalize the value.
byer - a cow house
{**cam** (comb) - remains of an earthen mound}
carr - flat marshy ground
chisel - bran
choups - heps [sic], the fruit of briars
clag - to adhere or stick together
cope - to barter or exchange
cope or coup - to empty or turn out
coul - to scrape earth together
cow-wa - come away
crine - to shrink, pine
crying - weeping
daft - foolish, stupid, insane
darking - listening obscurely or unseen
dene - a dell or deep valley
dight - to dress, to clean
doff - to undress
don - to dress
dowp - a carrion crow
draf - brewer's grains
drawk - to saturate with water
dreerood - a long and weary road
dub - a pool
an ear or a niere - a kidney
elsin - an awl
ennanters - in case of
fell - a moor or common
fettle - to make ready
flacker - to flutter or quiver
flaid - frightened
flit - to remove from one dwelling to another
{**fog** - aftermath i.e. grass which springs up after the
hay-crop}

fond - silly, foolish
forse - a cascade
froating - anxious unremitting industry
fusin - nourishment
gait or **gate** - a path, a way, a street
gait for cattle - the going or pasturage of an ox or cow through the summer
gaiting - a sheaf of corn set up on end to dry
gar - to oblige to do any thing
garsil - hedging wood
{**gavelock** - an iron lever}
gear - stock, property, wealth
gears - horse trappings
gill - a small valley or dell
{**gimmer** - a ewe sheep}
glair - mirey puddle
glif - a glance, a fright
glore - to stare
gob - the mouth
goping - as much as both hands can hold, when joined together
gouk - a cuckoo
grain of a tree - a branch
grape - a three pronged fork for filling rough dung
greeting - weeping
groats - shelled oats
grosers - gooseberries
hames, h'yawms - the two pieces of crooked wood, which go round a horse's neck to draw by [plus a footnote: This is pronounced 'yawmes', with the aspirate H before it.]
{**hard corn** - wheat and maslin}
haughs, holms - flat ground by the sides of rivers
haver - oats
haver-meal - oat-meal
{**heck** - lower half of a door, also an inner door}
hell or hail - to pour
heft - a haunt

hemmel - a shed for cattle, &c.
hindberries - raspberries (*Rubus Idæus*)
hipe - to rip or gore with the horns of cattle
hogg - a young sheep before it be shorn
hopple - to tie the legs together
{**howk** - to make a hole or cut earth with a spade}
howl - hollow
humbling barley - breaking off the awns {beards},
with a flail or other instrument
huse - a short cough
ings - low wet grounds
inkling - an intimation
kāve - to separate with a rake and the foot the short
straw from corn
kemping - to strive against each other in reaping
corn
{**kemps** - hairs amongst wool}
ken - to know
kenspeckled - particularly marked, so as to be easily
known
keslop - a calf's stomach salted and dried to make
rennet
{**kevel** - a large hammer for quarrying stones}
kite - the belly
kittle - to tickle
lake - to play
late or lait - to seek
leam - a flame
leif - rather
lemurs - ripe nuts that separate easily from the husk
letch - a swang, or marshy gutter
lib - to castrate
{**lick** - to beat, to chastise}
lig - to lie
ling - heath (*erica vulgaris*)
lingey - active, strong, and able to bear great fatigue
linn - a cascade
loach - a leach

{looking corn - weeding corn}
lop - a flea
lop-loach - the leach used by surgeons to draw blood
lowe - a flame
{lyery - abounding with lean flesh, esp. on the buttocks}
mang - barley or oats ground with the husk, for dogs and swine meat
{maslin - mixed grain esp. rye with wheat, also bread made of mixed corn}
maugh - a brother-in-law
maumy - mellow and juiceless
meal of milk - as much as a cow gives at one milking
mel-supper - a supper and dance given at harvest home
mis-tetch - bad habits
moudy-warp - a mole
neive - the fist
neivel - to strike or beat with the fist
nolt or nout - neat cattle
piggin - a wooden cylindrical porringer, made with staves, and bound with hoops like a pail; holds about a pint
plenishing - household furniture
prod - a prick
pubble - plump, full: usually said of corn or grain when well perfected
quickens or quicken grass - a general name for all creeping or stoloniferous grasses or plants, which give the farmer so much trouble to eradicate
rated - approaching to rottenness
{reins - balks of grass land in arable fields}
rice - hedging wood
rife - ready, quick to learn
rift - to belch; also to plow out grass land
rowting - bellowing of an ox
runch - a general name for wild mustard, white mustard, and wild radish

samcast - two ridges ploughed together

sare - much, greatly: as sare hurt, sare pained

{**scaling** - spreading mole hills or dung}

{**scallions** - young onions}

{**seives** - the articulated rush}

sheer - to reap or cut

{**shive** - a slice of bread &c.}

sipings - the drainings of a vessel after any fluid has been poured out of it

skeel - a cylindrical milking pail, with a handle made by one of the staves being a little longer than the rest

skelp - to slap, to strike with the open hand

skirl - a loud and continued scream or shriek

skugg - to hide

{**slape** - slippery}

{**slocken** - to quench thirst}

smash - to crush

snell - sharp, keen: as snell air

soss - to lap like a dog

spāit of rain - a great fall of rain

spāned - weaned

spurling - rut made by a cart wheel

stark - stiff, tight, thoroughly

stee - a ladder

steek the heck - shut the door

steer - a three years old ox

steg - a gander

stell - a large open drain

a stint - in stocking grass land is equal to an ox or cow's grass

stirk - a yearling ox or heifer

storkin or storken - to grow stiff: as melted fat cooled again

stot - a two years old ox

stour - dust

strippings - the last part of a cow's meal, said to be richer than the rest

swameish - shy, bashful

{**swarth** - sward, the surface of grass land}

{**swathe** - a row of mown grass, as left by the scythe}

syde - hanging low down

syke - a small brook

syles - principal rafters of a house

tawm - a fishing line made of hair

team - to empty a cart, by turning it up, to pour out

tewing - teazing, disordering, harassing

threave - 24 sheaves of corn, &c.

as tite - as soon

titter - rather, sooner

trod - a beaten path

twea - two

twibling - slender, weak

unletes - displacers or destroyers of the farmer's produce

wankle - uncertain

{**ware-corn** - barley or oats}

wattles - teat-like excrescences which hang from the cheeks of some swine

whang - a leather thong

whig - soured whey with aromatic herbs in it, used by labouring people as a cooling beverage

whye or quey - a heifer

win - to get: as winning stones, to get stones in a quarry

wizened - dried, shrivelled, shrunk

{**yaitings** - single sheaves of oats}

yaits (aits) - oats; hence probably gaitings from yaitings, single sheaves of oats

yak (ayk) - oak

yal - ale

yammer - to cry like a dog in pain

yan (ane) - one

yance (ance) - once

yap - ape

yarnut - arnut, earthnut

yat - gate
yaude - a horse
yedders - slender rods that go along the top of a
fence, and bind the stakes together
yerd - a fox earth
yerning - rennet
youl - to howl like a dog
yuke - to itch

Again, there is much here that is not in current use,
though some recognisable common terms receive
their first mention e.g. **bumble-kites**, **clag**, **tewing**.
Apparently, there are rather more Norse-derived
words here than in Kennet e.g. **lop**, **lowe**, **neivel**.
But if we consider purely those words with
agricultural relevance, we have a considerable list of
Norse-based terms: **beck**, **carr**, **fell**, **forse**, **garsil**, **gill**,
holms, **ings**, **haver**, **kenspeckled**, **ling**, **nout**,
rowting, **skeel**, **snell**, **stee**, **steg**, **tawm**, **threave**, **whye**
and **yaude**, which suggests a considerable
conservatism in face of the assumed disruption of
population the process of enclosure implies.
Without exact detail on where Bailey (and Kennet)
obtained their words, the lists are difficult to
evaluate; they agree only in their variation from
standard English, and (surprisingly?) from later
Durham pitmatic, but this very variation may reflect
some practice or bias in the collecting of words in
these cases that we know nothing about.

For the post-agricultural (industrial) era, there are
two important printed word-lists for the County,
that of Dinsdale (1849) and that of Palgrave (1896).
Dinsdale covered that portion of the Tees from
Middleton to Darlington, taking in the area North of
the Tees some 9-10 miles, basically the triangle
Darlington - Bishop Auckland - Barnard Castle. To
the West of Egglestone, Dinsdale notes,

36

pronunciation and terminology seemed to change, perhaps to a more traditional or 'highland' form e.g. **kirk** for <u>church</u>. But on the middle Tees, some familiar words were being recorded for the first time e.g. **aye, bullets** (sweets), **cannily, ettle, fairin', fash, galloway, gotherly, honey** (<u>hinny</u>), **how-way, kelter, mebbe, scumfish, tatie,** etc.; some are likely contemporary coinings or favourites, others probably of long pedigree e.g. the Norse-based **ettle**. It is exactly on the middle Tees that Viking influence might be expected, but this list may be more typical of emergent industrial speech, with the Tees connected by shipping with similar regions to the north, and coal-mining spreading in the west of the county.

In Palgrave's splendidly titled *List of Words & Phrases in Everyday Use by the Natives of Hetton-le-Hole in the County of Durham* (1896), the full weight of industrial influence on the language is demonstrated, for Hetton had had its pit since 1819, and throughout the County coal was becoming a traditional way of life. Palgrave is particularly detailed on children's matters: games, rhymes and slang terms, but equally records adult language with a fascinating authenticity, noting ruefully that 'bloody' is "to be heard several times in every sentence from certain individuals...." In this list, a majority of words are recognisable: **chimla** has replaced **lum**, a talk is a **crack**, and folk equate Geordie with a miner. A high proportion of these words are still recognised in the East of the County, at least among older people.

It may seem that major immigration into the County in the 19th century intensified or at least changed the non-standard element in the speech, though an underlying shift towards standard grammar seems evident by the end of the century. New-comers, though a major force in the pits and bigger towns, seem usually to have adopted or modified rather than displaced the dialect of the land that gave them work. Indeed, practical work considerations would ensure the perpetuation of a ready-made tested vocabulary in all technical matters. Tyneside speech was undoubtedly a main element in this Durham pit talk; but that already mixed speech probably modified further in what in turn became settled, local conditions. A useful note of this process is Jack Lawson's autobiography *A Man's Life*, published first in 1932. He writes thus of Boldon Colliery ca.1900:

"Its population consisted of people from every part of the British Isles, some of the first generation and some of the second, all boasting they were Durham men, though their parents spoke the dialect or had the accent of the distant place of their birth. Many of my Durham friends may not know it, but the fact is that, although we are all now Durham men and proud of it, not all of us by any means are native to the soil. Few can trace far back to a Durham lineage. True, the immigration slowed down, and then stopped in the early years of the twentieth century. Marriage and time have now almost obliterated the old county and national landmarks, and made them one people. But at the time of which I write there was a combination of Lancashire, Cumberland, Yorkshire, Staffordshire, Cornish, Irish, Scottish, Welsh, Northumbrian, and Durham accents, dialects, and languages. All these and more tongues were to be heard in a marked way; and not only that, but the families in each group gravitated together and formed a common bond....
"It was a polyglot population, and the Durham dialect, so marked among the children, did not hold unrivalled sway among their elders...." [ch.5]

This last comment is revealing, for it indicates that children influenced each other more to a consistency of speech than parents influenced them; their acute hearing and accurate miming, along with their own pressures to reach a youthful standard could be a major unrecognised factor in the perpetuation of Durham dialect. The divergent origins of the adults in this new population was certainly marked: a quick glance, for example, at a random street (German Row) in the 1871 census of Seaham Colliery gives us some 60 adults (over-18s) born inside County Durham but some 68 born outside the County. Of the 60 from within Durham, only five were actually born in Seaham; of the others, 18 came from Northumberland, 22 from the Tyne area, and 28 from elsewhere e.g. Ireland, Wales, Cornwall, Cumberland, etc. Through the birth-places of successive children in one family, we can see a marked tendency for the mine-workers to move around from pit to pit, sometimes making almost a yearly change of abode. This fluidity of population within the area may have reinforced rather than weakened the use of dialect, for there would have been a need for an accepted common speech, especially in the work-place, for sheer safety reasons, and this in turn made it likely that common speech would be based on regional mining talk - for which 'pitmatic' has become the accepted term.

As regards population, the 20th century has been altogether more stable, reinforcing changes and decisions made in the 19th century, and yet more destructive of dialect in some ways as more subject to processes like education. To return to Jack Lawson:

"There are no strange dialects now, because there are no strangers from other parts, for, as is well known, the county cannot even employ all its own. There is only one

39

dialect now, and only Durham people. The melting-pot process is complete." [ch.6]

Place and work were certainly influences for consistency of speech; the more so as new housing reflected more stable jobs, but also important may have been concepts of class. Thus John Green (*Tales & Ballads of Wearside*, 4th edn, 1885, pp.293-4) notes a "Mr Greenwell, who, though an educated gentleman, invariably spoke with a strong Tyneside burr", as though dialect and education were incompatible. It is quite possible that sectors of the Victorian ruling class considered dialect a useful class-marker, for distinctions of speech, as of dress, housing, morality even, were in effect desirable and helped define and so keep people 'in their place'. There would thus be little pressure to moderate dialect from above, and Palgrave notes that the 'natives' themselves were liable to modify their speech to different class contexts, as though as much aware of these different worlds as their 'betters' were.

A similar quasi-conscious effect is noted by Paul E. Kerswill in his article "Social and linguistic aspects of Durham (e:)". This looks at the difference between use of a rising and falling diphthong in words like 'day', and the emergence of a pure vowel in its place. Kerswill notes that the pure (i.e. later or smoothed) vowel is typical of "women, as well as of the kind of 'polite' or 'corrected' speech used by men employed, for instance, in service industries as clerks and shop assistants or as salesmen," (presumably in imitation of what is considered as superior/standard English); whereas the diphthong is typical of "men engaged in manual work." (p.18) Sexual and occupational roles may thus affect attitudes to and experience of dialect, with the possibility of changes in adulthood (p.21); it has seemed to me that face-workers in the 20th century were likely to speak with a broader accent, as though a marker of adult and work status. Women, alternately, may have been only too vulnerable to the prestige of fine language.[5]

To return to Kerswill: Ideally, it would be possible to distinguish between a rising diphthong ('home' - <u>hyém</u>/<u>yem</u> - North Durham and Geordie?), a falling one (<u>híem</u> - most of Durham), and a monophthong (<u>hohm</u> - from the influence of standard English) - but even this simplified picture is blurring with the upheavals and mobility attending unemployment now. For net emigration in the mid-20th century, and the loss of much heavy industry now looks set to have a far greater impact than 19th century immigration.

While work and class may have been influences tending to conserve dialect in the past (at least for the manual male worker), schooling seems to have been a formidable anti-dialect force, intentionally or unintentionally. National primary schooling, introduced around 1870, did not overtly outlaw dialect (in the way it stopped Welsh being spoken in Wales). But many saw it as a strong influence for standard English:

"The decline [in dialect] would set in with education easier of attainment and would be hastened from 1870 onwards by compulsory education. Many of us remember being told to speak properly and drop the 'Weardale twang'. No dialect words were in the school books, nor were any ever written and this alone was sufficient to

---

[5] see Pauline Lynn 'The influence of class and gender: female political organisations in County Durham during the inter-war years' *North East Histroy* 31 (1997) 43-64.

bring about its decline. Some schoolmasters did their best to ridicule it out of existence, describing it as coarse, vulgar and gawkish."

[John Lee *Weardale Memories and Traditions* (Consett, 1950) p.222]

The indifference shown to dialect in much 20th century schooling looks set to become positive opposition with the announcement (early 1993) that 'proper' spoken English is to be made part of the National Curriculum. (Imagine telling Australians, Ameri-cans or Canadians to conform in this way: their varieties of speech, after all, all derive from the ancient regional differences of dialects in this country. On first meeting a Russian in the mid-60s I was surprised to find him talking good *American* English.)

But schooling also had less predictable effects:

"As we were put into higher classes we were taught to read by the phonetic method, that is to split the word in syllables and pronounce each to form the word."

[Fred Wade *The Story of South Moor* p.75 re early middle C20th.]

It is to this mode of teaching that we might trace examples of 'spelling pronunciation' that are still apparent in the County and have helped to modify certain vowel sounds. Thus, when dialect 'iu' for 'oo' (long o̱) fell before standard English 'oo', what developed was a new form of the vowel, a lengthened 'oo', and not the short standard English equivalent at all (book, cook etc). By contrast long 'a' (not spelt 'aa' but 'a-e' etc.) was not so affected. 'Fakade' for 'façade' is another example. (This possibility of spelling influencing pronunciation was first noticed in the 1920s by Harold Orton.)

But if dialect is at risk from schooling, it may be at greater risk from its own image. It is seen as indelibly linked to 'working class status' and with it a traditional/reactionary life-style; and the instinct today is to let all this die a peaceful death, unmourned and unregretted. But this unkind and unnecessary verdict is surely based on a historical fallacy, for industrial workers were simply preserving, encouraging and modifying a type of local speech rooted firmly in a thousand years of North-East language development: their dialect is both the historic and the living language of the whole region, and it is dangerous to regard it as the preserve of any one group, class, generation or political persuasion.

The tight local (work) community that supported dialect is disappearing, and the group work-base, sense of identity, and stability of population that is useful to any local standard (and reciprocally helps affirm that identity) is disappearing; the modern office worker has to relate to a wide section of the public (as individuals) and adopts smart dress and smart speech, preferring to think of him- or herself as part of the standard English ambit, communicating with their own national fraternity along many a motorway and down many a fax. With the decimation of heavy industry, this sort of 'up-grading' looks increasingly attractive - that or 'emigration' - and neither augurs well for the future of dialect. Pronunciation, already noted as beginning to conform in the 1920s (perhaps from the effect of primary education), has continued to move closer to standard English (e.g. _bone_ than _bien_, _night_ (nite) than _neet_), and the range of vocabulary also has shrunk seriously in the last half century (as noted by Shields 20 years ago); grammar (in which field Northern English acted as a model for Modern

English) is almost entirely standard, and when people speak of 'dialect' today, they seem mostly to mean accent or 'twang'.

But although much can be attributed to local indifference of centralised aggression, factors like the development of technology also play a role. The spread of plastic as a material has had an effect in pushing out a range of treasured words: all wicker work (corve, creel, cawel, etc) has disappeared in favour of plastic shopping bags; wood, leather, natural cloths, glass, have in many cases fallen to artificial substitutes, and a whole spread of craft words will fall with them. The terms special to the mines are likely to disappear similarly now the pits are no more, as detailed agricultural vocabulary did before. Even the bairns are likelier to sit in front of the T.V. than be out combing hedges and ponds; and the many children's names for birds, animals, insects and especially games are likely to be forgotten. The computer (at work or at play) and the modern office context are unlikely to provide much support for traditional dialect except in monitoring its dissolution.

And so it is that major factors - industrial decline, education, technological shifts, and personal inclination - seem set against the retention of dialect. And the process is undoubtedly speeded by the way dialect is everywhere excluded from serious practical and official use. TV, radio, films, books, national newspapers all present us with standard English (or Anglo-American) while ignoring (and thus actively discouraging) dialect, or reserving it for semi-jokey slots like local weather forecasts. The enlightened but intense schooling of our day has no practical room for dialect. Nor has officialdom with its forms, nor any of the paperwork of everyday modern living. Dialect may even be deemed a bar to employment. No doubt, people want Durham to look and feel modern and progressive; but playing down dialect and risking severing another strand of regional continuity is not, in my opinion, a viable way to achieve this. Now, if ever, is the time dialect needs a little encouragement and cosseting. For we need to remember that language is something we make and use, and should have a say in. To present it as immutable (as though some unchanging punishment of the angels at Babel) is only to attempt to disguise the systems of control and change that do operate within human language all the time.[6] For it is clear that official contempt does not reflect the reality around us. 'Standard English' is spoken by as little as 5% of the population.[7] Arguably it is not a true living language at all. It is a fixed convenience, like Latin before it, which served as a practical international mediator or super-language: useful, nationally and internationally, but as a tool of written communication, of a specialised culture and scientific precision; it is at root limited and inflexible, non-oral and impersonal, and it would be

---

[6] Is it correct for a reality-engineering class even to think in terms of 'encouraging' dialect? Undoubtedly language is one of the dominant factors in defining reality, and with it, the proper concept of 'a human'. The 1980s have seen the spread of a slightly sub-standard English (dubbed 'Estuary English'), allied to right-wing views on every subject, which may give a political turn to the decline of dialect. Yet it seems pointless to legislate for dialect (in the way that Welsh local authorities insist on doing for Wales); rather there is a need to re-evaluate the role of dialect and lend it some positive credence, as a counter-balance to the many discouragements it receives, not least the belief that dialect is somehow inferior English.

[7] see V.K.Edwards *The Grammar of English Dialect* 1984 p.32

safer regarded and taught as a second language,[8] for that is what it is to the millions of dialect-speakers in this country: something to be learned as well as, not instead of one's own speech. Might some of the problems experienced with literacy in this country be resolved if this basic fact were taken into account, instead of persistently trying to present an alien standard as normal?

Now it may seem that by presenting the case for dialect I am inevitably suggesting a 'fossilization' of speech. Not at all. Speech will continue to develop and find new means of expressions, new words, new connotations (overtones) for old words etc, and in Edwards' opinion (p.31) the inflexions and grammar of spoken English are continuing to simplify themselves all the time. The invention of new words, usually denigrated as 'slang', has been typical of at least the urban experience of the last 200 years. **Kitty** (a lock-up), **skilly** (porridge), and **bullets** (sweets) are North-East examples, but standard English is shy of such terms, and often they have a limited life even in local popularity. A more traditional way of coining new terms was compounding, the combining of two standard words to express a new concept.[9] Currently, though,

---

[8] There seems to be some local recognition of dialect and standard English existing as parallels. Thus <u>nebby</u> has come to mean 'nosey' after the example of slang based on standard English; and <u>clart about</u> is used as an equivalent to standard English slang 'muck about'. That is, a dual language situation is recognised, with transfers from one context to the other. In general, I have noted that dialect speakers are uneasy about seeing their speech written down in any phonetic approximation; they have been taught to associate written form with standard language.

[9] My prize goes to 'raad-haader' or road-holder, for a car (originally CB slang?), with 'star-heed' for a Philips screw

youngsters are likelier to copy TV or adopt the fashions of American street-talk for their private usage.

In this situation of flux, what I suggest as important is simply that we should cease to exclude dialect as an influence on the future development of language in the North-East and bring it back into the main-stream of language thinking, for dialect is not a local aberration, a curiosity with no current relevance, but a valid version of English, with a pedigree as old or older than the supposed standard, whether we grace our version with the name 'pitmatic' or 'Durham pit talk' or call it (inaccurately) 'Geordie' - maybe we should go simply for a wider 'English of the North-East'?

---

a close second. Technically these are 'kennings' or puzzle-compounds, much appreciated in their own day by Viking and Anglo-Saxon (like the sinister 'sky-yelper'). In similar traditional mode are the compounds 'shackle-bane' (wrist), 'monifeet' (centipede), 'horn-top' (snail), 'queen's-heed' (postage stamp), 'slap-heed' for a stupid or forgetful person, 'joinedy-up thinking' for adult intelligence (on the model of 'joined-up writing?), and the C19th 'likeness' rather than the pseudo-Greek 'photograph'. There was a movement in the mid C19th to revive native compounds with words like 'folk-lore', 'star-craft' etc., cf. American 'ice-box' for fridge, German 'Fernsehen' for T.V. etc. But in England the desire for a quasi-privileged 'opaque' terminology in technical and professional spheres ('jargon') has prevailed. See further Raymond Williams *Keywords* (1976) s.v. 'folklore'.

Guide to the Development of Northern Pronunciation

Explanations:
OE = Old English, the language of the Anglo-Saxons in England, used as a writte medium from the 8th to 11th centuries. The two principal dialects are West Saxon and Anglian (Northern).
MidE = Middle English, as spoken between the 11/12th century and the 15th century. Less stable than Old or Modern English and with important regional variations.
Southern = Modern Southern English, the basis of 'Received Standard', 'Standard English', 'Queen's/King's English' etc.
monophthong = a pure or single vowel
diphthong = a compound vowel, in which two vowel sounds are slurred together.

1. Development of Long Vowels

a: (long 'a')
OE a: was preserved in MidE(Northern) as a:, while in MidE(Southern) it became o:
e.g. OE *hām* ('home') becomes MidE(Northern) *ham(e)*, MidE(Southern) *home*.
OE a: > MidE(Northern) a: becomes Mod.Northern a: (i.e. is preserved) in a few particular words
e.g. *nah* ('no'), *taa* ('toe'); but for *craa* ('crow'), *naa* ('know') see under 3. Diphthongs, below.
In most cases MidE(Northern) a: subsequently broke to give the diphthong i+a or i+e
e.g. *bien* ('bone'), *hiam / yam* ('home'), *stian* ('stone'), *biek* ('bake'), *giet* ('gate') *tweea* ('two'), *tiaties* ('potatoes') etc. This diphthong has some variation in itself: in Geordie the first element is reduced e.g. *spyéd* ('spade'); the first element of the diphthong is

48

usually 'i', but in some words in the south and west of the County it approximates 'e'.

Other variants:

Southern pronunciations are also found

e.g. o: (pronounced "oh") in *bōt* ('boat'), *rōd* ('road'); also the Southern diphthong a+i

e.g. *baik* ('bake'), *plait* ('plate').

For Southern o:, the pronunciation o+a is sometimes found, also that of ö (German 'o' umlaut, the vowel in English *sir, purr*)

e.g. *ro-ad* ('road'), *röd* ('road'), *nö* ('no') (these could be attempts to approximate Southern 'o', or spelling-pronunciations).

In a few cases, a short OE 'a' apparently did not lengthen in MidE(Northern) and subsequently break

e.g. *makk* ('make'), *bakk* ('bake'), *gamm* ('game') but these may be better explained as a later shortening of a long vowel or diphthong back to short 'a' - *makk* is recorded by Meriton in the C17th.

æ:/e: (long æ/e)

OE æ: (front 'a') merged with e: (long 'e', the vowel in *air*, but could also be rather like the 'eh' in *hate*, compare French *fête*) to become e:, and was then fronted to i: (pronounced 'ee')

e.g. 'wheel', 'eat', 'each', 'feet', 'guizer', 'street', 'sea' etc.

Variants:

There is a slight tendency for e: to break in ModNorthern (esp. in the south of the County) to the diphthong e+i

e.g. *feeat* ('feet'), *eit* ('eat'); in the case of *hiad* ('head'), *eit* ('eight'), there may by the survival of an older diphthong, unless these are spelling pronunciations.

In some cases, e: was fronted and shortened, giving 'i' -

e.g. *fritt* ('fretted'), *imti* ('empty'), *frind* ('friend'), *siv'n* ('seven').

i: (long i)
OE i: and y: (a rounded vowel like French 'u') had merged in MidE to i: (pronounced 'ee'), which is preserved in some words in some areas (esp. the west of the County):
e.g. *deed* ('died'), *ee* ('eye');
but in the majority of cases, presumably through the effect of southern English, i: broke to give the diphthong a+i
e.g. *skai* ('sky'), *ais* ('ice'), *bait* ('bite'), *raid* ('ride'), *main* ('mine') etc.
Variants:
the diphthong a+i was later sometimes monophthongized to a:
e.g. *Aa* ('I'), *drahving* ('driving').
OE short 'i' was lengthened before 'ht' but not diphthongised in general, leaving i: ('ee')
e.g. *leet* ('light'), *neet* ('night'), *reet* ('right');
sometimes diphthongisation to e+i occurred
e.g. *reit* ('right'), *feit* ('fight' - W/N County); cf. pronunciation of 'e' fronted to 'i'; but often Southern a+i is heard in this position also.

o: (long o)
OE o: broke in Northern to i+e
e.g. *biek* ('book'), *dien/diun* ('done'), *liuk* ('look'), *fiul* ('fool'), *neuk* ('nook'), *tiooth* ('tooth') etc. (There is some variation in the second element of this diphthong throughout the County.)
Variants:
In some cases o: became i: ('ee')
e.g. *dih* ('do'), *ti* ('to').
Before 'r', o: can dihpthogize to oh+a
e.g. *moar* ('moor'), *poar* ('poor').

In Southern, o: (oh) became u: (oo), and this
pronunciation (esp. the long vowel form, without
much tendency to shorten) is found in Northern too,
possibly reinforced by spelling pronunciation
e.g. *book* ('book'), *cook* ('cook'), *boot* ('boot').
But in both Southern and Northern this can then be
shortened (short 'oo')
e.g. *gud* ('good')
Alternately the long u: ("oo") pronunciation can
diphthongise to oo+uh
e.g. *cuel* ('coal'), *huel* ('(w)hole')

u: (long u)
OE u: was preserved as u: ('oo') in Northern
e.g. *broon* ('brown', OE brūn), *doon* ('down', OE
dūne), *hoo* ('how', OE hū), *coo* ('cow', OE cū), *poond*
('pound') etc.
Variants:
In Southern, u: became diphthongized to 'aw' (a+u)
as in 'brown' etc; this is sometimes found in
Northern now, but also a form o+u, which may be a
spelling-pronunciation
e.g. *bo-unce, o-unce.*

2. Short Vowels

OE a/æ merged to become the short front 'a' vowel
(represented here by 'æ')
e.g. *kæstl* ('castle'), *kæt* ('cat'), *fæde(r)* ('father', OE
fæder), *wætte(r)* ('water', OE wæter)
Variants:
In many cases short OE 'a' lengthened in MidE - see
above under long a:. This did not happen in
Northern before 'th', 'f', or 's' e.g. *bæth, græft, glæss*.
OE 'a' and 'o' before 'n' became Northern 'an'
e.g. *rang* ('wrong'), *lang* ('long'), *strang* ('strong')
but there are a few exceptions
e.g. *onny* ('any'), *monny* ('many').

51

Occasionally 'æ' is fronted to 'e'
e.g. *efter* ('after'), *hev* ('have'), *hez* ('has'), *thenkz* ('thanks'), *wesh* ('wash'), *esh* ('ash')
The combination 'ar' + consonant becomes long a:, much as in Southern
e.g. *aam* ('arm'), *yahd* ('yard'), *waam* ('warm' - which pronounced "wawm" in Southern).
The combination 'al' + consonant becomes long a: (as opposed to Southern 'or' sound)
e.g. *aad* ('old'), *aa/aal* ('all'), *baal* ('ball'), *kaad* ('cold'), *taak* ('talk'), *waak* ('walk'), *caa+caal* ('call')
but there are a few exceptions/alternatives
e.g. *bawld* ('bold'), *awld* ('old'), *sawld* ('sold' - perhaps indicating a modern form, as *selled* would be expected); and in the west and south of the County, pronunciations *corf* ('calf'), *cawd* ('cold') are found.

e.

OE short 'e' continues as 'e'
e.g. 'met', 'sent', 'defend'.
Variants:
Occasionally 'e' is raised to 'i'
e.g. *rint* ('rent'), *inj'n* ('engine'), *frish* ('fresh'), *stritch* ('stretch'). *iliven* ('eleven'), *git* ('get' - in west of County)
Occasionally this secondary 'i' is lengthened
e.g. *weel* ('well'), *reed* ('red').
Occasionally 'e' retracts to 'a'
e.g. *varry* ('very'), *varnai* ('very nigh/nearly'), *harrings* ('herrings')

i.

OE short i/y are preserved as 'i'
e.g. 'bin', 'finger', etc.
Variants:
Rarely an 'uh' sound develops: *wup* ('whip'), *skwurrul* ('squirrel').

52

In Northern, 'i' does not lengthen before nd/mb
e.g. *blinnd, finnd, climmb* (as opposed to Southern
'blaind' etc., though this is increasingly the Northern
pronunciation also).
In Southern and Northern, 'ir' + consonant becomes
'uh', as expected
e.g. buh(r)d ('bird')
but also in Northern it can become long a:
e.g. *waarse* ('worse'), *waak* ('work')

o.
OE short 'o' remains 'o'
e.g. 'body', 'box', 'frog'.
Variants:
Kolb records this vowel as slightly fronted in
Geordie.
Final 'ol' + consonant becomes or/aw
e.g. *rawl* ('roll'), *gawd* ('gold'), *fawk* ('folk')
though Southern long o: ('oh') is also found here.

u.
OE short 'u' is preserved in Northern as 'u' (short
'oo'), not as 'uh' as in Southern
e.g. *bootte(r)* ('butter')
Variants:
There is no lengthening in Northern of 'u' before 'nd'
e.g. *foon(d)* ('found'), *groon(d)* ('ground') - as
opposed to the Southern diphthong a+u ('ow');
occasionally the diphthong oh+oo is found
e.g. *bo-und, so-und* (a spelling-pronunciation?).
The combination 'ul' became u: ('oo')
e.g. *shoother* ('shoulder') - though this pronunciation
is now becoming rare.

3. Diphthongs
Most diphthongs result from the breaking of a long
vowel. Some examples not dealt with above are:

MidE ai/ei usually becomes smoothed to long e: (as in *fête*, like an 'ay' sound)
e.g. *brēn* ('brain'), *dē* ('day'), *bēt* ('bait' - or pronounced 'biat', ?by association with long a:); sometimes this is shortened
e.g. *fent* ('faint');
sometimes the diphthong seems preserved or restored as a+i
e.g. *stra-it* ('straight'), *a-it* ('eight').
MidE 'au' became long a: in Northern
e.g. *lā* ('law'), *raa* ('row'), *naa* ('know'), *snaa* ('snow'), *kahz* ('because'), *saas* ('sauce'), *craa* ('crow');
but before 'nt' it becomes 'æ'
e.g. *ænt* ('aunt'), *chænce* ('chance'), *grænt* ('grant').
MidE 'ou' becomes a+u ('aw') rather than Southern long o: ("oh")
e.g. *glaw* ('glow'), *graw* ('grow'), *fawe(r)* ('four'), *awt* ('aught'), *lawp* ('lowp/leap'), *lawse* ('lose')
The diphthongs 'ew' as in 'few' and 'oi' as in 'boil' are pronounced alike in Southern and Northern.

4. Unstressed vowels
These often level to an 'uh' sound e.g. *rabbut*, *pockut*, *hammuh* ('hammer'), *carrut*, *finguh* ('finger'), *Soondeh* ('Sunday') etc. - as compared to *pockit* in Yorkshire and the South.
Sometimes an unstressed vowel is in effect omitted altogether e.g. *coozn* ('cousin').

5. Consonants
There has been little change in the pronunciation of consonants in English, though the following examples are worth noting:
'h' tends to disappear: medially, it is no longer pronounced in English in words like 'night'; initially it is often omitted e.g. Northern *ham* becomes *hiam* becomes *yam* ('home'). Initial 'h' is usually

preserved in ModNorthern e.g. *hundred*, and often added e.g. *hadge* ('adze').

Similarly, 'r' in the middle and at the end of a word is weakened or not pronounced e.g. 'quarter', 'better'. An initial 'r' is prominent in Northumberland and Geordie, also in the combinations str-, dr- etc., and in the word 'iron'.

Final 'g' is usually ommitted e.g. *singin'*, *gannin'* etc. Medial 'g' (as in *finger*) is not separately enunciated.

In Northern, especially, a medial 't' is likely to alter, leaving a sort of glottal stop, e.g. *ma(tt)er* ('matter'), *boo(tt)er* ('butter'). Disappearance of medial 'd' is also recorded e.g. *han'l* ('handle').

In clusters of consonants, it is not unusual for one to become silent e.g.*kæsl* for 'castle', *groon* for 'ground'. Intrusive consonants also occur: inital 'w', as in *wor* for 'our' and medial 'v', as in *divaa* for 'do I'. Initial 's' (as in *scrush*, *scringe* etc) is of uncertain origin, and may in some cases be an authentic form (discussed in *Oxford English Dictionary*).

In OE (including Anglian) 'c' was palatalised before front vowels to give 'ch', as in 'church', 'cheese' etc; and 'sc' was pronounced 'sh', as in 'ship', 'short' etc. But in Old Norse (Viking), the 'k' sound was preserved and influenced first Northern then Southern English

e.g. OE *ćyrić* became English 'church', Scottish 'kirk'; and we have both 'ship' and 'skip' and 'skep' for container-like objects.

Viking 'k' for 'ch' is recorded in west Durham e.g. *sek* ('such'), *kirn* ('churn' - also south of County)

In OE, 'g' was palatalised before front vowels to give 'y', as in *ġiellan*, 'to yell'; but in Old Norse the sound was a hard 'g' (e.g. *goller* - to yell) and this was often restored in later English

e.g. we have both Northern *yet* and *giet* for 'gate' - the latter with the Norse meaning of 'road'.

There was a similar pair of variants sh/sk e.g. *shriek / skrike.*
OE 'cg' could become 'g' or 'j' e.g. *brig* (Durham) but *brij* (Geordie); the Durham pronunciation of 'cabbage' is *cabbish.*
OE cw became modern 'qu'; in Durham this sometimes simplifies to 'w' e.g. *wick* ('quick'), and in Cleveland changes to 'tw' e.g. *twilt* ('quilt').

6. Intonation
The intonation or variations in level of volume and melodic line of speech in a sentence may have a distinctive development in Northern English, though with no recordings prior to this century it might be hard to say what is traditional and what is owed to immigrant influence in the 19th century or developed locally then.
Typical of Northern is a rising intonation in the sentence, not just to convey a question but also surprise, emphasis, humour, perhaps even as a standard feature.
There is also a tendency to provide stock introductory and concluding words to emphasise the start/end of a spoken sentences, like "How!...", "Hexackly,...", "...., man.", "...., like."
In theory, it is possible by using a phonetic alphabet to put down on paper the nuances of dialect pronunciation, and further to add a graph-like line to represent intonation; but in practice, tape-recordings are a much better way to make a record of dialect speech: and it is here that a good local archive is very much needed at present. There is much scope here for any local enthusiast, school, club etc., to make a most useful contribution.

Word List

Abbreviations:

< derived from
> giving rise to
ċ pronounced 'ch'
cf. compare
C'land Cumberland
conj. conjunction
Dan. Danish
D'm Co. Durham
Du. Dutch
E East Co.Durham
EA East Anglia
F feminine
Fr. French
ġ pronounced 'y'
Gm. German
Ice. Icelandic
Ire. Ireland
M masculine
MidE Middle English
MidEN Middle
English (Northern)
Mids. Midlands
Mod. Modern
ModE Modern
English
N North Co.Durham
N'd Northumberland
N.E. the North-East
neg. negative

Newc. Newcastle
O Old
OE Old English
(Anglo-Saxon)
*OED Oxford English
Dictionary*
ON Old Norse
ONorthumb. Old
Northumbrian
onom. onomatopoeic
(imitative)
pl. plural
p.p. past (= passive)
participle
pres.p. present
participle
pret. preterite (past
tense)
pron. pronounced
S South Co.Durham
sg. singular
s.v. listed under
Swed. Swedish
T Tyneside
W West Co. Durham
West'd Westmoreland
Yorx Yorkshire
ð = th
þ = th

Sigla for the sources used

NE = North-East region
D = County Durham
T = Tyneside/Geordie
N/S/E/W = North/South/East/West of Co.Durham
numbers indicate era:
1 = pre-1815
2 = 1815-1915
3 = post WW1

NE1
John Ray *A Collection of English Words not generally used* (London 1674). Early dialect word list, Northern words, not specifically Co.Durham.

John Ray *A Collection of English Words* 3rd edition 1737 - revised by author, and enlarged with information from Francis Brokesby, rector of Rowley, E.Yorks, and other (e.g. Cumberland) informants.

NE2
John T. Brockett *A Glossary of North Country Words* (Newc., 2 vols, 1846); large work, using printed sources plus original material for the Newcastle area.

D1
Bishop Kennet's Etymological Dictionary; BL MS Landsowne 1033; includes a range of North country words, and some specified as 'Dunelm.' i.e. Durham. Not printed, though used in compiling Wright's *Dialect Dictionary*.

John Bailey *General View of the Agriculture of the County of Durham* (1810); includes glossary, concentrating on agricultural/practical terms.

D2

Cuthbert Sharp (ed.) *A Bishoprick Garland* (1834, reprinted Sunderland 1906). An uncomfortable range of texts with little editorial detail.

Wm Brockie *Legends and Superstitions of Co.Durham* (Sunderland, 1886). Contains some passages and phrases in dialect.

T1

Edward Chicken *The Collier's Wedding, A Poem* (1764); written 1720 in Newcastle. Includes the first printed passages in 'Geordie'.

T2

Thomas Wilson *The Pitman's Pay & other poems* (2nd edition 1872). Includes glossary prepared by the author, referring back to early C19th.

J.P.Robson *Songs of the Bards of the Tyne* (Newcastle ca.1849); includes glossary.

J.E.Hull "A Grammar of Tyneside", *The Vasculum* 8 (1922) 55-60,105-7, 117-21. Based on material relating to the period 1870-90.

D.Embleton *Local Dialect Dialogues* (ca.1897); Geordie, esp. medical.

H.F.Fallaw *The Tyneside Tongue* (Gateshead 1915)

T3

Scott Dobson *The Geordie Dictionary* (Newcastle 1974)

Mike Shields "Dialects of North-Eastern England", *Lore & Language* 10 (Sheffield Univ., 1974) 3-9

(T3)
George Todd *Todd's Geordie Words and Phrases*
(Newcastle 1977)

S2
Frederick T. Dinsdale *A Glossary of Provincial
Words used in Teesdale in the Co. of Durham*
(London, 1849)

G.M.Tweddel (ed.) *Rhymes and Sketches to
Illustrate the Cleveland Dialect* (Stokesley 1875);
includes a glossary.

S3
R.W.Blenkinsopp *The Teesdale Dialect* (Barnard
Castle, 1931)

Jean Crocker (compiler) *Accent on the North East:
Dialect jottings* (ca.1983, Darlington)

W1
'The Rookhope Ride' - C16th ballad recorded by
Joseph Ritson in 1792.

W2
William Egglestone *Betty Podkin's Visit to
Auckland Flower Show: An amusing narrative in
the Weardale Dialect* (Stanhope, 1876)
"..when yan gans away inted world yan gits yan's
een op'n'd"
William Egglestone *Betty Podkin's Letter ted Queen
on Cleopatra's Needle written ed Wardle dylect by
Peter Podkins, Jun.* (London, 1877)

W. Herbert Smith *Walks in Weardale* (Claypath,
Durham, 1883). Various general information
including list of dialect words (pp.90-96)

E2
John Green *Tales & Ballads of Wearside* (4th edn, London 1885); includes a few texts from Sunderland.

F.M.T.Palgrave *A List of Words and Phrases in Everyday Use by the Natives of Hetton-le-Hole in the County of Durham* (English Dialect Society vol.74, 1896). Reprinted Gateshead, 1997.

E3
Information from Seaham, 1990s, including general post-war word usage.

N2
Alexander Barrass, *The Pitman's Social Neet* (Consett. 1897, reprinted Seaham 1993).

N3
Fred Wade *The Story of South Moor* ("pitmatic", pp.187-90). Typescript at Durham Central Public Library.

a' - see ALL / **Aa** - see I / **aal** - see ALL

aback - 'behind' S2; **abacker** E2

aboot - 'about' T2,N2,E2,S2; "that'll be aboot it!" - 'you're right' E3

aboon - 'above' D1 (+**abeun**),S2; **abyoon** E2; **abuin** T2; **abi'en**, **abeain** W2 [OE ābufan]

abreed - 'spread out' S2 [OE ābrǣdan] cf. **breed**

acrun - 'acorn' S2

addle - 'to earn' NE1,S2; **adlings** 'earnings' D1 [OE edlēan 'a reward']

afeared - 'afraid' T3

aflaid - 'afraid' T2; cf. **flay**

afore - 'before' T2,N2,S2,T3; **afwore** W2; **aforelang** 'before long' S2; **fore** T2,N2

agane - 'against' S2 (+'before'),T3; 'for the time when' W2; **agyen** 'again(st)' T2

aglee - see **ajee-y**

AGREE: **gree** T2,S2,NE2

ahaad - 'hold' T3 ?noun cf. HOLD

ahint - 'behind' T2,E2,T3 [OE æt-hindan] cf. **behint**

aiblins - 'perhaps' T2; **ablins** NE2 [< able]

aigre - 'sour' S3 [Fr.]

aik - see OAK

airts - 'corners' W2; **airt/art** 'corner, region' D1 [Gaelic aird]

ajee-y - 'crooked, twisted' E2; **ajee** S2; "aal jee-wy" T2; **ajee-wye** E3; **aglee** 'awry' T2; [OED s.v. agee] cf. **jee**

ALL: **a'** T2,N2 (+**aal**),W2,W3; **aal** E2,N3; **oh** W2; **awl** T2,N2; **aal-o-bits** 'all in pieces' S2; **aalreet** 'alright' T3; **aareet?** 'hello' E3

amaist - 'almost' S2

amang - 'among(st)' D1,T2,S2,W2 etc; **mang** T2

amell - 'between, among' D1 (+**ameld**) [cf. Dan. imellen 'between']

ananters - 'in the event of' S2; **ennanters** 'in case of' D1,NE2,S2; **anauntrins** 'if so be, if perchance' NE1

AND: **en'** W2,N2,N3; **an'** T2,S2
ane - see one
anenst - 'opposite to' S2; **nenst** 'beside' T2, 'towards, in respect of' NE2; [OE <u>on</u>+<u>emn</u> 'at a level with']
ANYTHING - see **owt**
arf - 'afraid' NE1,NE2; **earfe** D1; **arfish** S2,NE2; [ONothumb. <u>arg</u> + ON <u>argr</u>]
argie - 'argue' T3; **argify** E3; **argies** 'debates' T3
arles - 'advance on wages' NE1,D1,T2; **arles/earles** 'an earnest, servants' vails, etc.' D1 Kennet as Yorx [OFr. <u>arres</u>]
arnicks - 'bulbs of buttercup tribe' E2 [<u>arnica</u>]
arran-web - 'spider-web' S2 [<u>arran</u> <Fr]
arrish - 'edge' S3 [OFr <u>areste</u>]
ASHES: **ass** E2,S2; **axen** D1
ask - 'lizard or newt' E2,S2; **asker** NE1 [OE <u>āþexe</u>]
aswin - 'obliquely' S2,S3
atop - 'upon' S2; **atoppa** W2
atweah - 'in two' S2; **atwee** T2,W2
atween - 'between' T2,S2,T3
aud - see OLD / <u>aught</u> - see **owt**
aum - 'elm' S2; **awm** NE1
aup - 'mischievous child' S2 [?=ape]
Aw - see: I / **awd** - see OLD
awn - 'own' T2,S2; **awn/awin** D1
ax - 'ask' T2,S2,N2; pret. **axt** N2, **axt/ast** S2 [OE <u>ascian/acsian</u>]
axleteeth - 'molars' NE1,NE2 [ON <u>jaxl</u> 'molar']
aye - 'ever, always' D1,T2,W1; 'yes' S2,N2,E2 (+ **yis**),S2,E3 [OE <u>ā</u>, 'always'] cf. **why-aye**
ayont - 'beyond' T2,NE2

babby - 'baby' S2,T2,T3
back-end - 'autumn' S2;"back-end of month" E3; "back ower" - 'back again' E3; "back ower bob" - 'out of order, disorganised' S3; **backly** 'backward, late' S3; cf. **fore-end**

backward than <u>backwards</u>
backy - see TOBACCO
BADGER: **brock** T2,E2 [OE/Gael. <u>broc</u>]; **pate** D1
    Kennet as Northern, NE2 ; **badger-neet**
    'Friday night' E3
badly - 'unwell' S2; **bad** E2
bagie - see TURNIP
bain - 'ready, near' D1; 'willing, forward' NE1;
    "bainer way" - 'nearer route' S2 [ON <u>beinn</u>
    'straight, direct']
bairn - 'child' T1,T2,S2,N2,E2,W2,W3,E3; **bearn-**
    teams 'broods of children' NE1 [ON <u>barn</u> +
    ONorthumb. <u>bearn</u>]
bait - 'a packed meal/snack' N2,N3,E3; **bait-poke** 'bag
    for such food' T2,N2,E2 [ON <u>bæit</u>]
baith - see BOTH
bane - 'bone' S2; **beyn** T2; **beean** S2; **bane-fire**
    'bonfire' S2; **bane-grubbers (byen-)**
    'scrapmen' T2 [OE <u>bān</u>]
bang - 'to strike, excel, surpass' T1 (+'to rush'),T2,S2;
    'to shift by manpower' W2; [ON <u>banga</u>]
bank - 'hill' E2,T3; "at bank" - 'the surface level of a
    mine' N2,N3 [OIce. <u>bakki</u> 'ridge, eminence']
banty - 'bantam hen' E3
banward - 'a daisy' S3 as Upper Teesdale [OE
    <u>bānwyrt</u> 'bone-wort']
bar - 'barrier' N2; **barre** 'gate of a city' NE1,D1, 'gate
    or stile in Yorkshire' NE2 Brockett; vb. 'to
    shut a door' S2 [OFr <u>barre</u>]
barguest - 'foreteller of calamity/death' D2 [OE <u>gāst</u>,
    'spirit, ghost']
barley - 'to claim' D2,T2; "barley me the big 'un" E2;
    bargie T3 [?= by your leave]
barm-cake - 'fruit-cake' E3 [OE <u>beorm</u> 'yeast']
barrow - 'a grove' D1 [OE <u>bearu</u>]
bat - 'to strike a blow with the fist or hammer' N3; 'a
    stroke or blow' S2,N2,E2,T3 [Fr <u>battre</u>]
bate - see **bait**

bawks - 'cross-poles in a hen-house' D1; 'beams of
timber in a building' S2; **balks/bawks** 'poles
laid over a stable or other building for the
roof' NE1 [OE <u>balc</u> + ON <u>balkr</u>]

BE: **I is** is the expected form in D'm, e.g. **I's** NE1, **I'se**
D1, **Aw'se** S2, "A's shower" - 'I'm sure' E2; {<u>I</u>
<u>am</u> Mids, N.N'land, but <u>Aw'm</u> found in T2};
thou's S2; **they is** S2; **are/ aren't** T2, **er** 'are'
W2; **wiz** 'was' T2,T3 (+**woz**); neg. **wasint** N2;
wasn't T2; **war** 'were' T2; neg. **wa-n't** S2

beal - 'to roar' (like a child) S2 [OE <u>bellan</u> + ON
<u>belja</u>]

BEAT: pret. **bet** N2

BECAUSE: **kas** N2

beck - 'a stream' D1,S2,E2, 'a side-stream to a burn'
E3 [ON <u>bekkr</u>]

beeld - 'high fence to shelter cattle' D1; 'a shelter'
NE1; **biel** 'a place of shelter' T2 [cf. Ice.
<u>boele</u>]

beeld - see BUILD

beestlings - '(rich) cow's milk just after calving' D1
Kennet as Yorx (+**beeslings**),S2,T2,E3 [OE
<u>bȳsting</u>]

begock - see **gock**

behint - 'behind' T2,S2 cf. **ahint**

BELCH: **belk** (vb) S2; **bowk** T3; 'rush of air' N2,E3
(+**belch**); **boke** 'to belch, to be ready to vomit'
NE1 [OE <u>bealcan</u> + ch>k]

belang - 'come from, be born in' T2,W2,E2,E3
[=belong]

bellanned/bellant - 'poisoned by lead fumes' S3 as
Upper Teesdale [cf. Derbys. **bellon/belland**
'lead-colic']

belly-timmer - 'food' T2

ben - see BUT AND BEN

betterly - 'fine' S2

bid - 'to invite' S2,E2 [OE <u>biddan</u>]

bide - 'to abide, endure' T2,S2; 'stay, remain' E2 [OE
bīdan]

biddy - 'a louse' S2 [?< Gael. bîdeach, 'very small']

big - 'barley' D1,NE2 [ON bygg]; see also **byg**

BIND: pres. **binnd** S2,N2; pret. **band** S2,T2 (+**bund**)

bing - 'bin' S2

bink - 'bench' S2; 'stone bench' e.g. for milk-churns
D1,S3; **binch** 'wooden bench' S2 [variants
on ch/k]

birk - 'birch tree' S2 [OE berċ + ON bjork]

bit - as approx. measure S2,N2,E2,E3,T3 e.g. "a bit
coal", etc. [cf. **lot**]

BITE: pret. **b'yat** S2

biv - see BY

bizen - 'something enormous & frightful' T2; **byzon** 'a
shame, scandal' NE2 Brockett as Newc.,T2;
bizon 'example, shame' D2 [OE bȳsen 'sign,
marvel, example']

blackclock - 'cockroach' E2,E3,T3; clock - 'a beetle or
dor, a hot-chafer' D1,NE1; **clocks** 'black
beetles' T2,S2

blackie - 'a Black' E3

blake - 'yellow' S1 (+'bleak'); 'yellow or golden' NE2;
'butter-yellow' NE1,S3; **cow-blakes** 'dried
cow-dung used as fuel' NE1 [OE blac/blæċ +
ON bleikr; but cf. Irish blay 'light yellow'] cf.
blea

blare - 'to cry or roar' (of children, drunks, animals)
NE2; 'to weep' N2; 'to cry' T2.E2; 'to poke out
the tongue' S2; **blair** 'to cry out' T1; **blarey**
adj. 'noisy' (of an infant) E2 [cf. Du. blaren]

blash - 'to splash' D1; **blashey** 'wet/puddly' T2,S2;
'thin, poor' e.g. watered beer T2 [onom.]

blate - 'bashful' NE1 (+**bleit**),T2; 'shy' T2 [?OE blāt
'pale']

blather - 'to talk on' E2; **blither** T2 [ON blaðra]

blaw - 'breath' N2; **blaa** T3; "get thi blaw" - 'regain your breath' N3; vb. 'to blow' T2,S2 [OE blāwan]

blaw - 'blossoms' S2; **blo'** S2 [OE blōwan]

blea - 'bluish or lead-colour' NE2; 'yellow' D1 [?Fr. bleu, ?OE blēo, ?ON blár] cf. **blake**

bleb - 'blister' D1,S2 (+'drop of water'); 'bubble/mark on skin' E3; 'blister, bubble' NE1; 'to bubble' E2 [onom.]

bleck - 'dirty grease' esp. in pit, E2 [ON blek 'ink']

bleck - 'to shame' [ON blekkja 'to impose upon']

bleezer - 'a square of metal big enough to cover the fire place and used to create a draught when starting the fire' S3; "chaakin' on the bleezer" - 'chalking...' i.e. a couple not talking to each other E3 [= blaze-, ?<ON]

blinn - 'blind' T2; E3 only in "blinnd as a bat"

blish - 'blister' (noun) S2; **blush** noun/vb E2

blithe - 'merry' W1,D1 [OE]

blonk'd - 'disappointed' S2,NE2 [<blank?]

boggle - 'goblin' S2; **bogle** 'a ghost' T2; **boman** 'bogeyman' S2 [Celt. bwg, 'a goblin', Welsh bwg-]

bonny - 'handsome' T2, 'pretty/fine' S2,T2,E2,N2,W3; 'pretty' (used sarcastially) S2,N3 [Fr. bon]

boody - 'earthenware' N2; 'sherds' S2; **bowdie** 'a sherd' E2; **bowley** 'sherds, stones etc. used to build a bowley-house' S3; **bowdy-kite** 'pot-bellied' T2; 'deformed' T2; {**boody**, N'd, D'm, **bowdy**, E.D'm}

bools - 'bowls','a game like shot-putting' E2; **booled** 'rushed' T2; **bowled** T2; **boolers** - 'bike wheels with middle removed and net in place to catch lobsters' E3

BOTH: **baith** T2; **byeth** T2; **baath** D1; **beeath** S2 [MidEN bathe, OE bā twā]

bottles - 'medicine' E2

bowdy - see **boody** / **bowk** - see BELCH

brade - 'to vomit' S3; **braidin'** 'retching without
vomiting' T2 [OE bregdan 'to jerk']
braffen - 'horse-collar' D1 (+**braugham**),E3 as Yorx
[cf. Scot. brechan]
brag - 'a mischievous goblin' D2 cf. **barguest**
bran & **suw** - M/F of 'pig' T2
brass - 'money' T2,S2,NE2
brat - 'child's apron' S2,NE2,E3; 'a coarse apron, a
rag' NE1 [ONorthumb. cf. Irish brat, 'cloth']
brattles - 'thunderclaps' S3 [onom.]
Aw's bravely - 'I'm in good health' S2; "brave an'
blashy" (of weather) NE2
braw - 'a wild boar' D2
bray - 'to beat, thrash' S2,E2,E3,T3; 'to bray or beat in
a mortar' D1; **a brayin'** 'a beating/thrashing'
S2; **brays** 'blows, beatings' T2 [OFr. breier]
brea - 'riverbank/hillside' NE2 (+**broo**); 'a brae' S3
[ON brá 'brow']
BREAK: pres. **brick** N2, **breek** T2; pret. **brack**
T2,S2,W2; p.p. **brocken** S2,T2,N2,W2,T3;
"coming back brokkens" - 'to be penniless' E3
breckins - 'bracken' S2; **brecken/bracken** NE2 [cf.
Swed. bräken]
breed - 'to spread' E2 Palgrave as agric.; **breade** NE1
[OE brædan] cf. **abreed**
breeks - 'the lower habiliments' NE2; 'breeches' T2;
'trousers' T3 [OE bræcce + ch>k]
brent - 'steep' (e.g. of stairs) D1,S2,E2; **brant** NE1
[OE brant]
brig - 'bridge' S2,T2 [OE brycg + cg>g]
BRING: pret. **brang** S2; p.p. **brung** E2 Palgrave
(+**browt** - "but fetch is commoner")
brinkside - 'riverbank' E2
brock - see BADGER / **brocken** - see BREAK /
brossen - see BURST
BROW: thus W but E: **forred**; **bru** 'eyebrow', 'fore-
head' T2; cf **brae**

brownie - 'brown linnet' E2; 'any small brown bird' E3

bud - see BUT

BUILD: pres. **beeld** S2,T2,N2; pret. **belt** S2; cf. **byg**

bullet - 'a sweet' E2,T3,S3; "black bullets" E3; "Nelson's bullets" - 'a sweetmeat in the shape of small balls' S2

bum - 'bailiff' N2,T2

bummeler - 'bumble-bee' E2; **bummlor** T3; **bumbler** E3 [onom.]

bumble-kites - 'blackberries' NE1,D1,D2; **bummelkite** S2; 'brambles' E2 ["from its being supposed to cause flatulency when eaten in too great a quantity" (Brockie p.115)]; cf. **black-kites** (C'land)

bummin' - 'humming' NE2,T2; 'whirring noise' T2 [onom.]

bunch - 'to kick' S2,NE2; also as noun [?=punch; but cf. Du. <u>bonken</u> 'to thrash']

buntin - 'the cone of a fir tree' T2

buntin'd - 'lined with planks' N2; **buntings** 'rafts of imported timber boated up the Tyne': "Let's go hikey on the buntin's" NE2 [*OED*, <u>buntons</u> 'pieces of squared timber']

burn - 'a stream' D1,E2, 'a main stream' E3 [OE <u>burna</u>]

BURN: p.p. **brunt** 'burnt' T2 {W. **brunt**, E/N **burnt**}

BURST: pret. **brast** S2 (+**brust**); **brust** T2; p.p. **brossen** S2

bur-tree - 'elder' D2 (+**bore-tree, brown-tree**) D2 [cf. Scot. <u>boortree</u>]

bus - 'to dress' S2; **buss** T2; "bussing the tyup" - 'decorating end of year corf of coal with candles' T2 [prob. ON <u>búask</u> 'to ready' but cf. French, <u>busquer</u>]

buse - 'a (cow) stall' D1,NE2; **boose** 'an ox or cow-stall' NE1 [OE <u>bōsiġ</u>, ON <u>báss</u>]

bussie - 'bus station' E3; 'bus fare' S3

BUT: **bud** S2,W2; **eh bud** - 'well...' T2; **aabut** 'ah, but'
E2; **nobbet** 'only, just' T2,W2; **nobbut** T2,S2
(=nought but); **wobbit** 'well but' E2
but and ben - 'back and front parts of a 2 room
house' S3 [?<out/in]
butcher - 'stickleback' E2
bute - 'money equalising a barter/exchange of horses'
D1; **boot** NE2 [OE bōte]
BUY: pret. **bowt** T2,S2; **browt** [sic] T2
BY: **biv** before vowel S2,T3; **bin** E2,T2
byg - 'to build' D1 [ON bygja] cf. BUILD
byre - 'cow-house' D1,T2,S2,E2,E3; **coo-byre** S2 [OE
bȳre]

cabbish - 'cabbage' S2,T2,E3; "cabbish caskets" -
'cabbage stalks' NE2,E2,T2 [cf. Ice. kaskur
'vegetable']
cack - 'excrement' S2,E3; **cacky** (adj.) E3,T3 [ON
kökkr, 'lump', cf. Dan. kakke]
cadger - 'a beggar' T2, 'a packman or itinerant
huckster' NE2; **cadjun** 'begging, working as a
migratory seller' (esp. of pots?) N2 [OED as
itinerant dealer]
CALL: pres. **ca'** T2,N2 (+**caal**); pret. **ca'd** T2; 'to drive
(animals)' T2
caingy - 'peevish' NE2; **kaingey** T2; **cainge** 'to
whinge' NE2
caller - 'fresh, cool' S2,T2,E2 [ON kaldr 'cold']
cam - 'remains of an earthen mound' S2; 'rising
ground' E2 [ON kambr]
canches - 'stony obstructions to hewing' N2
(**kanches**); **canch** 'stone associated with coal
so both have to be hewed simultaneously'
N3 [cf.Mids. cank-stone]
cannot than can't - thus most N.E. but **canna**
W2,T2,T3, **cannut** T2,S2, **can't** W; E2
Palgrave says **cannot** used absolutely or
before vowel, **canna** before a consonant

70

canny - 'gentle' T2, 'fine' etc. N2; 'fair, careful, gentle' etc. S2,T2,E2,S2,E3 [MidE cunnand 'knowing, skilful, dexterous' (cf.canny = 'shrewd') < ON kunnandi, cf. Swed. kunnig - but alternately, see **canty**]

cannily - 'decently, gently, neatly, dexterously' S2, etc. (but also **canny** as adv. e.g. "gan canny")

cant - 'to overbalance' NE2,E2 [?< Du. kanten]

canty - 'lively, cheerful' T2,NE2 [cf. Du. kant 'neat, clever']

carl-cat - see **queen**

carlings - 'peas parboiled then fried' S2,NE2,E2,E3 [esp. eaten on Carling or Care Sunday; cf. ON kerling 'an old woman']

carr - 'flat marshy ground' D1,E3 (in placenames only); 'swampy hollow' NE2,S3; **carre** 'a hollow place where water stands' NE1; 'a flat marshy piece of land under natural herbage, usually lying at or near the foot of a bank' W2 [cf.Dan. kjær 'a marsh'; an alternative meaning, 'a rocky place' is also possible, cf. Welsh carreg 'a stone']

cast than throw [ON kasta] cf. **up-cast, kessen**

catched than caught E3,T2

cat-choup - 'brier hip' NE2; **cat-jugs** S2; **cat-a-jugs** 'wild rose hips' S3; **choups** D1 [choup a variant of hip, cf. Norw. kjupa 'hip']

cat-haws - 'hawthorn-berries' NE2,E2,E3

cavel - 'the place allotted to a hewer in a coal mine, by ballot' NE2, 'a working place in the mine selected by lot' N3; **kyevils** N2,E2; **kyevel** 'a lot' T2; {**cavel**, Scot, N'd; **cavil**, E.D'm} [?< ON kafli 'a piece of wood' / Du. kavel 'a lot']

cawel - chicken-coop D1 [ONorthumb. cawel 'basket']

ce- see **ke-**

CHAFFINCH: **sheelie** NE2,E2; **scobbie** E2; **chaffie**
E3; **spink/sphink** S3; **spink** S2 [spink prob.
onom.] cf. **gouldspink**
champion - 'great' E3; 'excellent' T3
chare - 'lane, alley' T2,T3; 'narrow street' T2
{Brockett as Newcastle/Bishop Auckland; E3
as York; *OED* as N.E.; Wright as N'd, D'm,
W.Mids} [?<OE ċierr 'turning']
chauldron/kauldron - 'coal waggon' E3; **chalder**
'coal waggon containing ca.53 cwt' NE2
[OFr]
chatties - see POTATO
chawvor - 'young person, pal' S3
checkers than draughts E2
checky - 'checked' e.g. "blue checky shirt" E3
chiel - 'a young person' T2,NE2 [?=child, or Romany
chal 'person']
childer (pl.) than children NE2,T2
chimla - 'chimney' E2; **chimli** T2,T3
chip - 'to trip up; a wrestling fall' [via Wright; cf.
Dan. kippan; ON kippa 'to pull, etc']
chirm - 'cooing of a bird' NE2,S2; 'chirping sound'
S3 [OE ċirm]
chisel - 'bran' D1 [OE ċeosel, 'grit' etc]
chist - see **kist** / **choups** - see **cat-choup**
chow - 'chew' (vb) T2,S2 (also noun),S3; 'a quid of
tobacco' T2,N2 [<chowk <ON kjálki
'jawbone']
CHRISTEN: **kirsen** T2,S2; p.p. **kirsten'd** T2;
kessenin' 'a christening' S2
CHRISTMAS: **Cursamus** T2, **Kirsmas** S2, **Kersmas**
etc NE2,W2; **Kessmus** S2; **Cursamus** T2; cf.
YULE
chucks - 'jacks' E3, 'a game originally played with
sea-snail shells and a marble' T3; [thus
Wright, chuck = sea-shell(?)]; **chuck** 'to
throw' S3

chucky - 'a chicken' S2; 'child-word for young fowl' E2,E3,W3 [onom.]; **chucky-eggs** W3

chucky - 'penis' E3; 'a hearty fellow' T2

CHURN: **kirn** (vb) S2; **kern** NE2 [ON kirna]

CHURCH: **chorch** T2; **kyrk** NE1, **kirk** (Barrass as Scots, but still used in C'land, and Durham in place-names); **kork** T2 [MidEN kirk, OE ċyriċe]

claes - see CLOTHES

clag - 'to cling or stick close' D1 (+**cleg**),T2,S2,N2,E2, N3,E3; 'to hit' ("Aa'll clag ye one")T3,E3; **claggy** 'sticky' S2,E3,T3; **claggum** - 'toffee' T2,E2, **clag-candy** NE1 [Dan. klag 'sticky', cf. OE claeġ 'clay']

clam/claime - 'to make stick, adhere' S2; 'to press, squeeze' NE2; **cleam** 'to glue together' NE1; **crame** 'to clamp and glue' NE2,S3 [ON klaeima]

clam/clammer - see CLIMB

clap - 'to stroke, pat' S2,T2 (+'to put onto'),E2; 'to touch gently, to fondle' NE2 [ON klappa]

clarts - 'street-mud' E2,E3,N3,T3; **clart** S2,S3; **clairts** T2; **clarty** 'dirty/muddy' S2,E2,E3,T3; "clartin' aboot" - 'mucking about' E3; **beclarted** 'besmear'd, bedaub'd' D1 [MidE biclarted]

clash - 'to rock, knock' E2,E3; 'to bang down' NE2,S2; 'to slam' T3; noun 'a chat' T1,NE2 [?onom.]

clashy - 'wet' (weather/road etc) S2 [OED = 'with bursts of rain']

claut - 'to claw' S2 [?<claw]

clavers - 'idle talk' NE2,T2 [cf. Gael. clabaire, Du. kalaberen]

clavver - 'clover' S2; **claver** NE2

clavver - see CLIMB

clay - 'a substance used by pitmen as a substitute for candlesticks' T2

claypy - 'scruffy/dirty' E3

cleä - 'claw' (noun) S2

cleg - 'horsefly' D1,S2; 'gadfly' NE2,T3 [ON klegg]

click - 'to clutch, catch (at)' E2.T3; **klick** 'to snatch or
catch up' D1,S2,T2, **click up** D1 Ray as
Lincs, E2; also noun, **click,** 'a rent/tear'
S2,E3,T3 [MidEN cleke]

CLIMB: pret. **clam** S2,T2; **clamb** NE2; **clammer** 'to
climb' S2; **clavver** S2, **claverin'** T2
[climb/clamber; clamber a new verb formed
in the C15th apparently from the pret. form
clamb]

clinkin' - 'splendid' N2 [cf. Scot. clink 'cash']

clivor - 'skillfull, properly' N2; 'in good health, well,
properly' E2

clocker - 'a broody hen' E3,T3,S3; **clocking-hen** NE2
[OE cloċċian 'to cluck', ON klekja 'to hatch']

clocks - see **blackclock** / **clog** - see **Yule-clog**

clogs - 'wooden-soled shoes' S2, 'shoes of leather and
wood' NE2

CLOTHES: **cloots** N2; **claes** T2,S2,N2,E2,E3; **cleeas**
S2; **clout** 'cloth/rag' S2, **cloot** E2, **claith** T2;
pudding-clout E3; **stick-and-clout** 'umbrella'
E2 [MidEN clathes]

CLOVER: see **clavver**

coäl-heed - 'idiot' E3

cob - 'to thump' D2; **cobbing** 'a beating' D2

cobble - 'flat-sterned clinker-built fishing boat' T3,E3
(+ cōble) {long 'o' more typical of Nort-
humb.?} [?Welsh/Breton ceubal/caubal;
cf.OE cuopel]

cobby - 'hearty/brisk' NE1,S2,T2; 'stout, high, proud'
D1; **cobby/coppy** NE2; "cobby as a lop" S2
[see OED cob sb.1]

cockle - 'to vomit' E3; 'to spit' T3; **cockly** (adj.)'sick'
E3

cod - 'cushion' T1; 'pillow' NE1; **kodd** 'a pillow box'
D1; **pin-codd/prin-codd** 'pin-cushion' NE2
[?Ice. kodde]

cogley - 'unsteady' S2,NE2,N3; 'of uneven motion' E2,E3; cf. **joggly**

coin - 'to turn from the straight' N3,T3; "coin the corner" E3 [Fr. coin 'corner']

COLD: **caud** NE2,S2,T2; **cawd** S2; **coad** W3; "a perishment o' cold" - '(in bed with) a cold' S3,E3

colley - 'child-word for cooked meat' S2,NE2 [?ON kolla 'cow']

COME: pret. **com** N2,S2 (+**cam**); **cam** T2 etc.; **comm'd** S2,NE2

corby - 'raven' S3 [OFr corbet]

corve - 'a whicker basket' e.g. for hauling coals in, N3; sg.**corf**, pl.**corves** S2,T2,N2 [Du. korf]

cotterels - 'coins' T2; 'a trammel to hang the pot on over the fire' NE1; **cottrils** 'coins, loose change' T2,T3; **cotterill** 'a split pin' NE2,E2, E3 [cotterel 'washer','pin' etc, < cotter 'pin, fastener']

coul - 'to scrape earth together' D1,NE2; **cowlings** 'bits raked together' S3 [Fr. cueillir]

coup - 'to overturn, tip up' D1 Bailey (+**cope**),T2, T3,E3 (+'to tumble'); "cowp thor creels" - 'do a somersault' N2, 'die' T2; **coup-cart** 'tippable cart, dung-cart' E2,E3; [Fr. couper]

COW: **coo** S2 etc.; pl. **kye** 'cows, kine, cattle' D1 (+**kine**),NE1,D1,S2,T2,W3 (+**kews**+**coos**) [OE cū]

cow-wa - 'come away!' D1 cf. howay

cowp - 'to exchange or swap' E2,S3,E3,T3; **coup** NE1 Ray; **cope** D1 Bailey,S2; **caup/kowpe** NE2 Brockett [ON kaupa, to buy/barter/ exchange; cf.OE cēapian]

crack - 'conversation' NE2,T2; 'talk, chat' N2,E2, E3,T3; 'talk, boasting' T2; "what's the crack on...?" - 'what's the news about (s.thing)' E3; vb. 'to boast' + noun 'news' [**crack**, cont.] NE2,S2; 'to talk boastfully' T2; 'someone best

at something' T2,N2 [onom.? cf. Dutch
kraaken, Fr. craquer 'to talk boastfully']
cracket - 'stool' T1,NE2,N2,W2,E3; 'stool to support
hewer at work' N2; 'stool with inverted-V
legs' E2,E3; **creckit** 'oblong stool' S2; [cf. Low
Gm. kruk-stool]
crame - see **clam**
cranch - 'hard, brittle substance' S2 [?=crunch]
cf.**canches**
cranky - 'tottering, unsafe' T2 Robson; 'poorly,
sickly' T2 Embleton [cf. Gm. krank 'ill', Du.
kreng 'lop-sided' of a ship]
cree - '(animal) pen, (pigeon) shed' E3 etc; **cray**
'hutch' E2 [ON kro, 'pen for lambs']
creel - 'basket for wool' S2; 'whicker basket' NE2;
fishing-creel 'basket for carrying fish in' E3
[OIr. criol 'chest' or OFr greille 'whicker-
work']
CREEP: pret. **crap** S2; p.p. **croppen** NE2
crine - 'to shrink' D1,NE2 [?cringe; cf.Gaelic crionan
'to lessen']
crouse - 'cheerful' T2,N2; 'brisk, lively, jolly' - "as
crowse as a new washen louse" NE1; 'brisk,
lively' NE2,T2; **cruse/crous** 'saucy, malapert'
D1 [cf.Frisian krûs 'free-growing, jolly']
CROW: **craw** S3,E3; **crake/cruke** S3; **dowp** D1,S3,
dope S2 [cf. Scot. dow 'pigeon']; **midden-
crow** NE2; {dowp, Common North except
Lancs}
crowdy - 'porridge' S2,NE2,T2,E2,E3,T3; 'poultry-
mash' T3,E3 [cf.Ice. groutr 'porridge']
cuddy - 'a donkey' T2,E2,E3; 'a horse' T3 Todd; 'a
left-handed person' S2; **cuddy-wifted** 'left-
handed' S3; **cuddy-wafter** 'a left-handed
person; a queer' E3; **cuddy-hunk** 'fishing
cord' E3; **cuddy-root** 'licorice' E3 [pet name,
[**cuddy**, cont.]

76

dim. of Cuthbert; but cf.Hindu <u>ghudda</u>,
Persian <u>gudda</u> 'ass' ?via Romany]
cundy - 'drainage ditch' NE1 (+**cundith**),E2; 'cleft,
hidey-place' E3; **cundeth** 'drainage ditch' S3;
'female genitalia' E2 [OFr <u>conduit</u>]
curran-berries - 'currants' etc. S2
currick - 'cairn of stones' NE2,W2,S3 [?Gaelic]
Cursamus - see CHRISTMAS
cushat - 'wild pigeon' D1; 'wood pigeon' S2,NE2
(+**kowshut**),T3,S3; **cusset** E3 [OE <u>cūscote</u>]
cushie - 'child-word for cow' S2,NE2

'd - 'the' W2; 'it' in **for'd** T2
dacker - 'uncertain, unsettled' NE2 [cf. Mid.Du.
<u>daekckeren</u>]
DAD: **da** E2; **deddy** T2; cf. FATHER
dad - 'a lump' T2; 'a blow or thump' NE2; 'a flat
blow' E3; **daad** T3; **dawd** 'a slice (of bread)'
E2; 'to hit', as "I'll dad thee lug" N3; **daddin'**
'beating dust out of pit clothes' N3; [onom?
cf. Scot. <u>dawd</u> 'a chunk']
daffle - 'to become senile' S2,NE2 [ON <u>dauf</u> 'deaf,
dull']
daft - 'fond, doting' D1; 'foolish, stupid'
NE1,D1,S2,T2 (+'thoughtless'),E2,E3 [OE
<u>gedæfte</u> 'meek']
daggy - 'drizzly' S2,NE2,S3; **dag** 'to drizzle' NE2; **deg**
'to moisten' NE2; 'to pour' NE1 [cf.Ice. <u>deigr</u>,
Swed. <u>dagg</u>, ON <u>döggottr</u>, and see *OED*
<u>daggly</u>]
daized - 'numb from cold' S2,NE2
darg - 'a day's work' T2; **darroc** NE2 Brockett as
Durham; **daurak** T1 [<<u>day-work</u>]
darkening - 'twilight' S2,NE2
darking - 'eavesdropping' D1,NE2
dather - 'to quake or shake' (with cold) D1 Kennet,
S2 (+variants); **dodthery** 'doddering' W2;
dothery/dothering 'shakey' E2,E3

daw - see **dow**

DEAD: **deed** T2,S2,NE2,T2,W3,E3; "deed folk" - 'the dead' T2

DEAF: **deef** NE2,S2; **deafely** 'lonely, solitary' NE1; **deave** 'to deafen' S2,NE2,E2

deas/dess 'outside stone bench' NE2; **des-bed** 'folding bed' N2, **desk-bed** E2 [OFr. deis 'table']

DEATH: **deeth** S2,T2,N2

dee - see DIE, DO

deek - 'look at! see!' T3 [Romany, dick]

delve - 'to dig' S2,E2 [OE delfan]

denched - 'queasy' S3

dene - 'a valley' D1; 'dell or deep valley' D1,NE2,E3; 'wooded hollow' S2,E2 [OE denu]

DEVIL: **de'il** T1; **deevil** T2,N2; **deeavel/divvel** S2; 'a safety device on a coal tub' N2

dickie-hedgie - see SPARROW

DIE: **dee** W1,NE2,T2,S2,T3 [ON döyja]

dike - 'ditch' N1; 'a hedge/fence' S2,NE2 Brockett (+'embankment'), E2,W2; 'hedge, ditch, wall' T3,E3; 'a dry hedge' D1 Kennet as C'land; 'any little pond or watering place' D1 Kennet as Yorx; **dike-loupers** 'trespassers' NE2; "gan ti th'dyke" - 'to take a pee', thus a diker 'an unofficial break' E3; {Wright gives =ditch as Yorx/Mids, =hedge as D'm/Cumbria} [OE dīc / Ice.dik]

dill - 'to allay pain' S2,NE2 [ON dilla 'to lull']

dinaa - see KNOW

ding - 'to beat, strike, knock' D1; 'to strike, surpass' NE2,S2 (+pret.**dinged/dang**); **dang** (pret.) 'pushed over' S2 [ON dengja 'to hammer']

edippy - 'addled' (esp. of a wild egg too aged to blow out) E3

dirl - 'to vibrate' T2,NE2 (+'to move round quickly') [?<drill]

dirt-birds - see SPARROW / **div,divvent** - see DO

DO: **dee** T2,N3 etc, **de** T2,N2, **dae** N2; **deea** S2; **dih**
E3; **div** T2,NE2,N2; **diz** 'does' S2,T2,N2,T3;
did 'do it' N2; p.p. **deun** 'done' N2,T3, **diun**
T2, **dune** S2; "she went done her shopping"
E3; neg. **dee'n't** 'do not' S2; **dinna** NE2;
dinna/dinnet T2 (+**dinn't**),S2,S3,T3; "A
dinna think't" E2; **dinyer** E3; **dinnot** S2;
divent T2,N2,T3, **divvin** T3, **divint** N3;
divent/dinnit T2; **doan't** E3; **dizna** 'doesn't'
NE2; **disent** T2; **didn't** T2; {<u>divvent</u> is a
Tyneside form; expected in D'm is <u>don't</u> +
centrally <u>dinnot</u> + W. <u>dunnot</u>, SE & Cleve
<u>deen't</u>} [forms with -v- may come from ON
<u>duga</u> (g>w>v), or from inverted form <u>do-I</u> >
<u>div-I</u>; Palgrave says <u>dinnot</u> used absolutely
or before vowel, <u>dinna</u> before consonant]
dobby - 'ghost or spirit' S2; 'local sprite' NE2;
'prankster or boggle' D2 [?<<u>Robert</u>]
docken - 'dock plant' NE2,D2 [OE <u>docce(n)</u>]
dodd - see FOX
Dode - 'George' T3
Doggy - 'West Cornforth' W3
dook - 'to bathe' S2; **douk** 'to duck, plunge
underwater' NE2 [=<u>duck</u> (vb)]
dorsent - 'daren't' T2,T3,E3
doubt - 'to think, suspect' E2; 'to doubt' T2; **doot** T2
[<Fr]
douce - 'snug, neat' T3; 'neat, sober' NE2 [Fr. <u>douce</u>]
dother - see **dather**
doving - 'dozing' NE2,E2; "dovered ower to sleep"
T2,E3 [ON <u>dofi</u> 'torpidity']
dow - 'to thrive' NE2,S2, **daw** D1; **dught** 'was able'
e.g. D1 Kennet "I did as I dught" [OE <u>dugan</u>
'to suit']
dowly - 'melancholy, lonely' D1,NE2,S2; 'miserable'
T2; 'dismal' N2; 'dull' E2; 'dull, sad' S3;
'lonely' S3 [ON <u>daufligr</u>, cf. Irish <u>doiligh</u>]

dowp - 'buttock' NE2 as Newc.; **dowpy** 'the youngest child' T2 [ON <u>daup</u> 'bottom'] for **dowp** = crow, see CROW

dozzen'd - 'spiritless, withered' NE2,T2; 'poorly, sick' S2; **dozzent** 'stupid' T3 [cf. ON <u>dúsa</u> 'to doze', <u>dasa</u> 'stupefied', and see *OED* <u>dozen</u>, vb.]

DRAGONFLY: **sanging-eather** 'the large dragonfly' NE2 (+**tanging-nadder, fleeing-eather**); "stangin' ether or flying adder" D2; **tenging-ether** 'large dragonfly' S2 [<u>eathor</u> = <u>edder</u> = <u>adder</u>, + ON <u>tange</u> 'a point']

drawk - 'to saturate with water' D1, **drack** NE2; **drawked** 'soaked'- "A've gotten drawked throu" E2; **draak'd** E3 [ON <u>drekkja</u>]

dree - 'lonely, wearisome' D1,S2,NE2; 'long, tedious' NE1; vb. 'to suffer, endure' NE2 [OE <u>drēogan</u> + ON <u>drygja</u>]

dreg - 'improvised brake' N2,N3; 'piece of wood or metal used to jam spokes' E3 [?=drag]

drite - 'to recite sing-song fashion' S2; 'to drawl' NE2

DRIVE: pres. **drahves** S2; pret. **drave** S2, **drov** E3

drouth - 'thirst' NE2,T2; **droothy** 'thirsty' T2,T3 [drought]

drucken - 'drunk' T2,S2,NE2 [ON <u>drukken</u>]

drumly/drumely - 'muddy' T2,NE2 (+'confused'); **druvy** 'muddy' T2, 'dirty, muddy' T2 [OE <u>drōfliċ</u> 'turbid, disturbed']

dub - 'a pool' NE1,D1,NE2

duds - 'ragged cothes' T2,NE2; 'clothes' E2,N3; 'working clothes' T2; 'best clothes' S3 [MidE <u>dudde</u> 'a garment' ?< ON <u>dudi</u>]

duff - 'fine coal or coal-dust' E2; **duffy** 'trashy' E2 [?C19th term]

dught - see **dow**

dunch - 'to run into with force, as, *the tubs dunched*' N3,E3 (of cars); 'to knock accidentally' S3; **dunsh** 'to crash' T3; **dunsh/dunch** 'bump

into' T3, 'to jog with the elbow' NE2; 'to
nudge or jog' E2 {Wright gives dunsh as
more Northerly form} [MidE <u>dunchin</u>,
cf.Mod.Dan. <u>dunke</u> 'to beat'; OE <u>dencgan</u> 'to
strike']

dwamy - 'sickly/faint' T2; **dwarmy** 'faint/languid'
E2,E3; "dwahm'd off" - 'dozed off' T2; **dwalm**
'a swoon' NE2 [OE <u>dwolma</u> 'confusion',
cf.Du. <u>dwelm</u> 'giddiness' etc]

an ear/a niere - 'a kidney' D1; **ear** S2,NE2 [MidE
<u>nere</u>, ON <u>nyra</u>]
EARTH: **eard** D1; **yearth** T2; **yerth** S2; **yarth** D1;
orth N2; **yerd** 'a fox earth' D1; **yearthly**
'earthly' T2, **yeardly** 'vastly' NE1 [OE <u>ġeard</u>,
ON <u>jarð</u>]
eath - 'easy' D1 [OE <u>ēaðe</u>]
eather - see DRAGONFLY
ebbs - 'sweets' S3 (as child's term)
ed - see IN; THAT / **eers** - see YEAR / **eesht!** -
see WHISHT
eftor - 'after' S2,T2,NE2,N2,N3 etc
ELDER - see **bur-tree**
eld-father, eld-mother - 'grandfather, grandmother'
D1 [OE <u>eald-</u>]
eldin - 'firewood' S2,NE2; **elden** 'fewel for the fire'
NE1 [ON <u>eldíng</u>]
eller - 'alder' S2,NE2 [OE <u>alor</u>]
elsin - 'an awl' D1,NE2 [MidDu. <u>elssene</u>]
en - see AND
endways - '?forwards' S2,NE2; **enways** 'endways' T2
cf.**heedways**
ennanters - see **ananters**
enter-common - 'open to everyone' E2
ENOUGH: **enow** W1 (+**enew/eneugh**); **eneugh** S2,T2;
eneuff T2; **eneeagh/eneeugh** S2; **u-nyoof** E2;
{<u>enow</u> probably literary rather than local}
er - see BE; OR

ettle - 'to arrange beforehand, contrive' T2,N3; 'mean,
   intend' NE1 (**+eckle**),NE2,N2,E3,T3; 'to try,
   attempt' S2, "A ettled to gan to Hetton" E2
   [ON _ætla_]
EVER: ivor N2; **ivver** S2,T2,W2,S2; **ivory** 'every' N2,
   iv(v)ery S2,W2, **iv'ry** T2; "ivery yen" - 'each'
   T2
ewlet - see OWL
Exactly... - 'Well, as I was saying...' E3
excepting that... - conj. E3
EYE(S): ee sg. S2,T2; **een** (pl.)T2,NE2,S2,T2,W2,E2
   (in set phrases); **ies** pl. N2 [OE pl. _ēagan_]

fad - 'a bundle of straw' NE2 (**+faud**), 'farmyard
   littered with straw, for keeping stock in' E2
fadder - see FATHER
fadge - 'small flat loaf' E3,T3; 'bun made out of spare
   dough left over when baker's tins have been
   filled' T2 [_OED_ as esp. Scots] cf. **stotty**
fain - 'glad' S2,NE2 [OE _fæġen_]
fairin' - 'present from a fair' S2,E3
fairly - 'steady' N3
FALL: pres. fa' T2; p.p. **fa'en** T2,S2
farand - 'manner, bearing'; **fighting-farand** 'ready to
   fight' NE1,NE2; **ill-farand** 'ill-looking' NE2;
   farantly 'handsome'; "fair and farant" NE1;
   aud-farand 'of children, when grave or
   witty, beyond their age' NE1; 'old-seeming'
   i.e. wise, of a youngster NE2,E2, **aud-farrant**
   S3; **farand-man** 'travelling merchant' NE2
   [OE _farende_ 'travelling'; ON _fara_ 'to suit']
farn-tickled - 'freckled' E2 [from supposed action of
   fern-seed?]
farther than _further_
fash - 'trouble' T1,T2,NE2,S2,E2,W2,N3,T3; vb.
   S2,NE2,E2 (e.g."he disn' fash the hoose
   mooch" - 'is seldom in'),S3 [Fr. _fâcher_]

FATHER: **fadder** S2,S3; **feathor** N2; **faither** T2;
feyther T2; **fahther** W2;
fadder/fayder/fayther S2 [OE f<u>æder</u>] cf.
Dad
faw - 'an itinerant tinker' T2; **faw-like** 'gipsy-like' S3;
fah 'a gipsy' T2; **faw-gang** 'troop of gipsies'
NE2 Brockett re N'land [< <u>Faa</u>, Scots gipsy
surname]
fea/fow - 'to cleanse or empty, as to *fea a Pond, a
Privy* etc.' D1 [ON <u>fága</u>]
feak - 'to twitch'? T1 [?<ON <u>fjúka</u>]
feal - 'to hide' NE1,S2,NE2 [ON <u>fela</u>]
feck - 'portion' N2,E2; 'a good quantity' (C'land); 'the
most or greatest part' D1 Kennet as Yorx
[?OFr <u>pek</u> 'a measure'; or ?< <u>effect</u>]
feckless - 'weak, feeble' T2; 'helpless' NE2,E2
[=effect-less]
fedder - 'feather' S2
feed - 'any sort of food e.g. sprats for mackerel' E3
feg - 'a fig' S2,T2
fell - 'a moor or common or hillside' D1,W1; 'rocky
hill' NE2 [ON <u>fiall</u> 'mountain']
feltered - 'rough, shaggy (of pony)' S3; 'matted' NE2
[<<u>felt</u>]
femmer - 'weak, delicate, frail' S2,NE2,N3,E2,E3,T3;
'fragile' T3 [ON <u>fimr</u>]
fend - 'to make a living' T2,E2; 'manage, cope'
S2,NE2,N2; **fendy** 'industrious' S2, 'capable'
NE2; "a fendable fellow" D1 Kennet as
Northern; **fend** (noun) 'defence' W2,
'endeavour, effort' S2, 'a livelihood' T2 [OFr
<u>defendre</u>]
fetch than <u>bring</u> E2
fettle - 'to set or goe about anything, to dress or
prepare' NE1; 'to make ready, prepare'
[**fettle**, cont.]
D1,S2,T2; 'to repair, mend, fix' NE2,D1
Kennet as Northern,N2,N3; also noun '(good)

state, condition, mood' S2,E2,T3,E3; "what
fettle?" a greeting... "Oh, canny" E2,G3,E3
[OE fetel 'belt', ON fetill 'strap, bandage']
fick - 'a struggle' S3 [cf. *OED* fick/feague 'to thrash'
possibly a slang use of Du. vegen 'to sweep,
wipe']
FIGHT: pret. **fit** 'fought' N2, **fowt** T2; p.p. **fitten** N2
FIND: pres. **fin**' T2; pret. **fand** T2,S2,N2,W2, **fund**
N2; p.p. **fund** S2,N2,E2
fippence - 'fivepence' T2,S3
fir-apple - 'fir-cone' S2
fix-fax - 'tendon of neck' S3; only re animals NE2
[from resemblance of muscle to hair strands?
MidE fex 'hair', cf. fax 'hair' (D1 Kennet as
Northern)]
fizz - 'to hiss' T2,S2; **fizzle** 'a faint crackling noise'
N3 [onom.]
flacker - 'to flutter or quiver' D1,NE2; 'to flinch or
turn back' N3, "never flackered" E3;
flackered 'worn out' N3; **flecker** 'to flutter'
S2 [MidE flakeren, ON flokra]
fladges/flatches - 'snowflakes' E2 {Wright notes flag
as Scot, N'd, Yorx, flatch as E.D'm} [OE
flaċea (via Junius), cf. Du. sneflage, MidE
flaw]
flannen - 'flannel' N2,S3
flaun/flawn - 'a custard' D1 Kennet as Northern;
flawm/floam/flarm 'flattery' S3 [*OED* flam]
flay/fley - 'to scare' S2,T2 (+noun),E2; p.p. **flaid** D1
Kennet as Northern,T2; **flayed** T2,S2,N3;
flay-crow 'scarecrow' S2 [ON fleyja 'to
frighten'] cf. AFRAID
flee - 'to fly' S2,T2,NE2,N2; **fleein**' N2,T3 e.g. "a
helicopter fleein' aboot" E3; p.p. **flowen** T2;
[**flee**, cont.]
fleein'-eather 'the large dragonfly' NE2; **flee**
'a fly' S2 [OE flēon, ON flya]
FLING: pret. **flang** 'flung' T2,S2; p.p. **flung** S2

flit - 'to move house' D1,E2,T2 etc. [ON _flyttja_]

flond - 'tempestuous' S3

flucker - 'a flounder' T2,NE2 (+**fluck, jenny-flucker**) [OE _flōc_]

flutter-by - 'butterfly' E3

flyte - 'to scold, quarrel with' S2,NE2 [OE _flītan_ 'to strive, contend']

foalfoot - 'coltsfoot' E2

fogge - 'long grass remaining in pastures till winter' NE1; **fog** 'grass growing after hay-cut' D1,S2 [cf. Scot. _foggage_]

foisty - 'musty' S2,E3,T3; **foist** 'fusty' NE1, 'to smell musty' NE2 [OFr. _fuste_]

FOLK: **foke** than _people_; **fwoak** W2

fon - see FOR

fond - 'silly, soft' T2,T3; 'silly, foolish' D1,S2,NE2,E2,E3; **fondie** 'a silly person' NE2,E2 (e.g."Thou's a fondie"); 'a game' N2 [MidE _fon_ 'a fool']

footy - '(game of) football' E3

FOR: **fon** before vowel E2; **fo/fer** S2; **fur** E2

force - 'waterfall' D1,S2,NE2,E3,T3 [ON _fors_]

fore - see **afore**

fore-end - 'early part' S2; 'Spring' NE2; cf. **back-end**

forbye - 'besides' T2,NE2,N2,N3,T3; prep. & adv.E2 [cf.Dan. _forbi_]

FORGET: p.p. **forgetten** T3,E3

forky-tail - 'earwig' T3

fornénst - 'opposite' T2,NE2,N3 (**fernenst**), E2 (+'in relation to' (someone)), T3; **fonenced** 'beside' S3 [_fore_ + _anent_]

forthless - 'worthless' E2 [cf. OE _forðian_ 'to achieve']

fortnith - 'fortnight' E2,N2; **fotnith** S2

fow - see **fea**

fower - 'four' N2,T2,E3

FOX: **tod** NE2 Brockett as N'land; **fox** + **dodd** T3; {_tod_ esp. Scot.}

fozy - 'light and spongey' NE2; 'unsound' (vegetable) E2,E3; **fozzy**, of root veg. gone soft E2 [cf. Du. voos, Norw. fos, 'spongey']

fra - see FROM

fratchy - 'cross-tempered, quarrelsome' NE2,E2 as Newc. [onom.?]

freet - 'to fret' S2; noun 'a fright' S2

FREEZE: pret. **froz** T2; **frozzin** p.p. 'frozen' T3,E3

fremd - 'far off, not related to, strange, at enmity' NE1; 'strange, unfamiliar' S2,NE2,E2,W2; 'a strange or stormy (day)' S3; "fremd wiv" - 'estranged from' T2 [OE fremde]

a fresh - 'a thaw' E2 as rural

fret - see **sea-fret** / **frev** - see FROM

fridge - 'to rub' S2 [see *OED* fridge/frig]

froating - 'anxious unremitting work' D1,NE2 [?OFr froter]

FROM: **fra** T2,S2,W2,S3; **frae** T2,W2,S2,E2,T3; **freh** N2; **frev** S2,S3,T2 [ON frá]

frosk - 'frog' D1 as Northern,S2,W2 [OE frosc, frox, frogga]; cf. TOAD

full / fullen - 'house-leek' D2

fullick - 'a blow with great force' N3 [full + lick]

fulmart - 'polecat' W2; **foomart** S2 [OE fūl-mearð]

funnin' - 'joking' T3; **funny** 'merry' T2

fusin - 'nourishment' D1 [OFr. foison]

fuzzball - 'mushroom' (*Lycoperdon borista* or puffball); **fusba'** NE2 [?<fozey]

gadgie - 'old man' T3; 'watchman' T3; **gadgey** 'tramp' S3 [?Romany gorjo, 'gentile']

gae - see GO

gaffe - 'cinema' T3,E3 (as old-fashioned) [Wright as 'music-hall, show' etc; *OED* as 'fair, place of entertainment' - C18th term]

gaffors - 'bosses' N2; sg. 'foreman' E2 [?<godfather]

gain - 'tolerably, pretty well' NE2 Brockett as N'land; 'expert', 'nearer', D1 Kennet as Northern;

"gainer way" - 'the nearer way' S2 [ON gegn 'straight, direct']

galloway - 'pony' S2,E2; **gallowa** W2,E3,T3; **gallower** N3 [breed from SW Scotland]

gallash - 'to mend shoes with leather' NE2; **galluses** 'braces' T3, **gallowses** S3 [Fr. galloches; but Wright suggests connected with gallows]

gam - 'game, sport' S2,N2,E2; vb. 'to mock' NE2; "mak gam of" S2 [OE gamen + ON gama]

gang - 'to go or walk' NE1 Chicken; **gan** T2,S2,W2,N2,E2 ("A's gannin doon..." but "A's gan to dae't"); **gannin'** (pres.p.) T2; "canny gannen" - 'good progress' S3; pret. **gann'd** E3; p.p. **gane** S2, **gaane** W2; **gyen** T2; **geyn** T2; **geean** S2; **gwan!** 'go on!' E3; **ganner** 'a (good) go-er' S2,S3; **ganger** NE2 [OE Ang. gangan + ON ganga] cf. GO

gansey - 'jersey' E3; **ganzy** S3 [<Guernsey] cf. Jarsey

gar - 'to make, cause or force' NE1; 'to compel' W1,D1 Kennet as Yorx/Northern,T2, NE2 Brockett 'in common use in all the Northern counties',W2,N3 [<ON gera]

garn - 'yarn' i.e.'thread' NE2,S2 [ON garn]

garsil - 'hedging wood' D1; garcil 'small branches to mend hedges' NE2 [cf. Swed. gärdsel 'fencing']

garth - 'enclosure/paddock' S2,S3,E3 as Yorx; 'small enclosure adjoining to a house', NE2 Brockett; 'yard, backside, croft' NE1,D1; **taty-garth** 'potato plot' E2 [ON garðr 'house and yard']

gat - see GET

GATE: **gait** - 'path, way, street' NE2,S2 (+**geeat**); the pasturing of cattle for the summer' D1 Bailey (+**yat**),'a right of pasturage' NE2; 'manner' T2; [**gate**, cont.]
'way, road, journey' E2,E3; **yett** T3; **gyett/yett** T3; **yat** 'a gate' S2,NE1 Ray (**yate**), T2 Wilson

(yett); yat-post D1 [ON <u>gata</u>: 'road/way' / ONorthumb. <u>ġæt</u>]

gav - see GIVE

gavelock - 'a pitch, an iron bar to enter stakes into the ground' NE1; 'an iron barr' D1 Kennet; **geavlick** 'esp. used by masons & quarrymen' NE2; **geaivlick** W2; **gyavlic** 'gavelock, crowbar' S2 [OE <u>gafeluc</u>, '?javelin']

GAWK: ('to stare') - **gaak** T3; **gwaak** T3; **gauve** 'to look...with an enquiring gaze' NE2

gay - 'fair, moderate' e.g. "a gay while" S2,NE2

gear - 'stock, property, wealth' D1,NE2; 'clothes, equipment' NE1; 'riches, trappings' T2,S2; 'tools' N2,T2 **(geer)**; 'belongings, equipment, tools' W2,S2; 'to dress' D1 Kennet as Northern [ON <u>gervi</u>]

geck - 'scorn, derision' e.g. "Dinna ye mak yor geck o' me" NE2 Brockett as D'm [cf. Du. <u>ghecken</u>]

Geordies - 'rustics' T2 Robson; 'miners' E2 Palgrave; **Geordie** = George T2 Wilson, NE2 Brockett, S2 Dinsdale; 'pitmen, Tynesiders' T2 Embleton; "The sailors belonging to the ports on the north-eastern coast of England are called Jordies" *OED* 1866 as first occurrence [< supporters of King George? i.e. Hanoverians, non-Tory; Scot. use <u>Geordie</u> to mean 'a guinea']

GET: pres. **git** S2,W2,W3; gerra 'get a' E3; pret. **gat** W1,S2,T2,N2; p.p. **getten** S2,N2,NE2,E2,E3,T3, **gettin** T3, **gitten** S2; **get** used absolutely: 'to get, manage, reach' E2 [MidEN <u>getyn</u> OE –<u>ġiten</u> p.p.]

gie, gien - see GIVE

gill - 'a small valley or dell' D1,S2; **ghyll** 'a ravine' E2 Palgrave as esp.Lake District; [**gill**, cont.] 'subsidiary valley to a dene' E2 (in place-names) [ON <u>gill</u>]

gimmers - see **jimmers** / **girn** - see GRIN / **girse** - see GRASS

gis-gis - 'a call to a pig' E2; **gissy** NE2; **gissy-pig** 'child-word for pig' S2, 'glutton' W3; **gissy** 'pig' T2, **guissie** E3,T3, **grice/grise** D1 Kennet as Yorx   [<ON gríss 'pig']

GIVE: pres. **gie** NE2,T2,S2; **gied** 'give it' T2; pret. **gav/gov** T2 (+**goh**),T3; **ga'** S2,T2; **gav** S2; **gov** N2,T2; p.p. **gien** S2,T2,W2, N2,E3; **geen** W2,E2,N2; "giv ower!" - 'stop that' NE2,S2,E2

glair - 'mirey puddle' D1 [OFr glaire, 'white of egg, sticky stuff']

gleg - 'to squint' S2,NE2 (**gley**); ?noun 'a glance' S2; adj. 'quick, clever' T2; **gledged** 'gaped' T2 [ON glegg 'quick-sighted', Swed. glia 'a glance'; and see OED s.v. gleg, gledge]

glent - 'to ricochet or glance off' S2; 'glance' T2; vb. 'to glint' W2; 'to glance' S2,NE2 (+noun); **glinted** 'peeped' T2 [cf. Swed. glänta]

gliff - 'a glance, a fright' D1; 'a glimpse, a fright' NE2; 'a sudden fright' T3; 'a glimpse' D1 Kennet as Yorx,S2,T2; vb. 'to startle' E2 [cf. Du. glippen]

glime - 'to glance slily' NE2, **glymin'** T2

glishy - 'bright' (weather etc) S2; **glisk** 'a transient light' NE2

glore - 'to glower, stare' D1,S2 [MidE gloren, cf. Swed/Norw. glora 'to stare')

GO: **gae/gee** NE2; pres.p. **gawin'/gaun** T2, gaan T2, **gi'en** W2; pret. **gaed** NE2 Brockett as D'm/N'land [OE gān]; pret. **yewd/yod** 'went' NE1,NE2 [OE ēode]; pret. **went** S2; p.p. **went** NE2,E3 [OE wendan] cf.**gang**

goaf - see gove

gob - 'the mouth' D1,T2,S2 (+**gab**),N2,E3,S3; **gobbin'** 'chattering' T2; **gobby** 'saucy' T2; **gob-stick** 'a spoon' NE2 [?Irish/ON /OFr]

by gock - expression of surprise or horror E2; **begock**
T2; **Gock!** S2 [gock for God?]
goke - 'apple-core' S2; **gowk** E2,E3,T3; **goke/gowk**
S3, 'the core of an apple, the yolk of an egg'
NE2 [cf. OE ġeoloca 'yolk'] cf. **gowk**
goldings - 'corn marigolds' NE1
goller - 'to shout, to speak in a boisterous or
menacing manner' NE2; 'to yell' N2 [ON
gaula]
gome - 'to notice, heed' E2; **gaum** 'to mind or look at'
NE1 Ray as Yorx; 'to understand' NE2;
gaum/goam 'to gaze or stare at in an indecent
way' D1 Kennet [ON gaumr 'attention']
GOOD: **gud** E3; **goodish** 'pretty good' S2; **good-like**
'handsome' S2, 'well-favoured' NE2
GOOSEBERRY: **grosers** (pl.)D1; **grozer**
T2,NE2,E2,W2; **gozzers** E3 (+**goggleberries**)
{grozer esp. N. of D'm + N'land; Scot. grozet}
[< Fr. groseille]
gore - 'a triangular patch' (e.g. of land) S2 [OE gara]
Gotham - 'Newcastle' T2 [from C16th satires on the
wise men (rather, fools) of Gotham]
gotherly - 'sociable, kind' S2,NE2,N2
gouk - see **gowk**
gouldspink - 'goldfinch' S2 [cf. Scot. gowdspink,
Swed. gulspink] cf. **spink**
gov - see GIVE
gove/goaf - 'the space remaining in a coal mine after
the removal of the coal' NE2 Brockett (**goaf**);
'area emptied of coal underground' N2
Barrass (**gove**); **gob-fire** E3 [ON gólf, 'a bay
of a barn, a space between wooden
supports'] {as 'segment of barn', survives in
Yorx, Lincs, Northampton, EA, as mining
term, N'd, D'm, Yorx, Lincs.}
gowk - 'a contemptible fellow', 'a fool' T2;
gowk/gowkie E2; **gawk** 'a clown' T2 [ON

gaukr 'a fool', probably same as following
word]

gowk - 'a cuckoo' D1 Kennet as N'land (+**gouk**),NE2;
Gowk-Day 'All Fools Day' D2 [OE geac, ON
gaukr] cf. **goke**

gowpin' - 'a double handful' T2; goping D1; "gowd-i'-
gowpens" T2 [ON gaupn]

gozzers - see GOOSEBERRIES

grain - 'branch (of a tree)' D1 Bailey,NE2; **grayne**
'clan/family' T3 [ON grein 'branch/fork']

graithe - 'to make ready or repair' S2,N3; 'to furnish
(with clothes)' NE2; **grath(e)** 'a hous or room,
to deck it or dress it up neat and fine' D1
Kennet [MidEN graythe, ON græiða]

grape - '3-pronged dung-fork' D1; **gripe** 'tool, fork'
T3, 'fork for lifting potatoes' E3, 'dung fork'
S3 [?< Fr. grapenel/grapon; ON græip]

GRASS: **girse** D1 Kennet as Yorx,S2; **gars/gurse** NE2
[OE gærs]

grave - 'to dig' S2,NE2 [OE grafan]

GREAT: **greeat** S2, **gert** W2, **girt** NE2, geut E3,T3,
greet T2; {expected forms: S: **geyt/gyut**;
N/W/G: **geet**; S/E: **gu(r)t**} [via metaphasis and
loss of 'r' in great]

gree - see AGREE

greet - 'to shed tears, weep' D1,T2,W2,E3; 'to cry, to
weep aloud' NE2 (+ pret. **grat**) [OE grētan,
ON gráta]

grey-bird - 'thrush' E2

GRIN: **girn** 'to twist the face' T2; 'to grin' D1 Kennet
as Northern; **gurn** 'to grin' N2; **girn**
NE2,S2,T2 [metaphasis of 'r' in grin]

GRIND: pres.p. **grundin**' 'grinding' T2,S2; pret.
grand S2

grip - 'a ditch, gutter' S2; 'gutter in a cow-house' NE2
[OE grype]

gripe - see **grape** / **grozer** - see GOOSEBERRY

grunge - 'to grunt' E2; **grune** S2; **grounge** 'to growl, as a dog' NE2

gud - see GOOD

guisen - 'to dry and contract' (of tubs etc) E2, **gizen** NE2; **geyzen'd/gizen** 'parched with thirst' T2; **guisen'd** 'tubs that leak through drought' NE1; **wizzend** 'dry-skinned' T2; **kizzen'd** 'parched' T2 {Wright gives gizzened as Scot, N'd} [ON gissen 'leaky']

guising - 'play-acting by people dressed up'; also vb. to guise E2; **guisers** 'masqueraders, fancy-dress revellers' S2,NE2,E3,T3 [cf. disguise, guise (from Fr)]

gully - 'a big knife' T2; 'farm-house or butcher's knife' NE2; 'a common hous-knife' D1 Kennet as Northern; 'carving knife or bread knife' S2,E2,T3 [possibly from gullet]

gwan! - see GO

hack - 'a mattock' S2; 'two-toothed pickaxe' NE2; 'a heavy pick' E2; **hadge** ?'adze,mattock' E3 [cf. OE haċċian, Du. hak, OFr hache]

hacky - 'dirty, filthy' N3,T3,E3; **hacky-black** 'pitch dark' E3; **haakie** 'pet name for cow' T3

hae - see HAVE

hagworm - 'adder' E?; 'large brown worm' S2; 'the common snake' NE2 [ON hoggormr 'adder']

hain - 'to conserve' (land, by enclosure) NE2; 'to hedge or fence' D1 (**hayne**); 'to shield, cover for' E2; 'take care of' W2,E3 [ON hegna 'to save/protect']

HALF: **hofe** W2; **hauf/hawf** S2

halse - 'throat' D1 [OE/ON heals 'neck']

hanckled - 'entangled' S2 [ON hanka 'to coil up']

handfast - 'a staple' S3

HANG: pres. **hing** T2,S2,N2,E2,W2; "hung on" - 'under way' N2; "hingin' on" - 'the time the pit begins to draw coals' T2

hansel - 'a deposit of money' NE2 Brockett;
    hanselled 'worn in' S3 [*OED* s.v. <u>handsel</u>
    'gift, pledge, trial' etc. OE/ON]
hant - 'a habit' e.g. "a nasty hant" E2 [=haunt < Fr.
    <u>hanter</u> 'to do frequently']
hap - 'a cover' + vb. 'to cover warmly'
    D1,NE2,S2,N2,E2,S3 (as vb.); 'an overcoat'
    T3; **happe** 'to cover for warmth' NE1;
    happing 'a coverlet' NE2 [?OSwed. <u>hypia</u> 'to
    cover']
happen - 'to meet (an accident etc.)' E2
har - 'small rain' D1; 'fog' NE2; **harl** 'a mist' D1,NE1
    [*OED* s.v. <u>haar</u> ?< Du. <u>hare</u>]
hardlies than <u>hardly</u> E3
hask - 'harsh' S2; 'coarse, harsh, rough' NE2 [MidEN
    <u>harsk</u>]
hat - see HIT
HATCH: **coal-hetch** E3 cf. **heck**
hatter/hotter - 'to shake' S2,NE2 [?Fr. <u>heurter</u>]
haughs/houghs - 'flat ground by the sides of rivers'
    D1 Bailey [OE <u>healh</u>]
HAVE: **hae** T2,N2,E2,S2 (+neg. form **hennot**); **heh**
    N2,T2, **heea** S2; **hev** T2,S2,W2 (+**ev**),N3; **hez**
    (3pres.sg.) S2,T2,W2; **hed** 'have it' N2, **hae'd**,
    het S2,T2; "you haven't to..." - 'mustn't,
    shouldn't' E3
haver - 'oats' D1 Ray as C'land,NE2; '(oat)meal' S2
    [ON <u>hafre</u>]
HEAD: **heed** T2,N2,W2,W3,E3; **heead** S2 [OE
    <u>heafod</u>]; **slap-heed** 'idiot' E3 ; **hede-wark**
    'headache' S2 [ONorthumb. <u>wærc</u> 'pain' cf.
    toothwark]; **heedways** 'head-on, forward' T2
HEAR: pret. **hard** W2,T2, **heeard** S2,W2, **ard** N2
heck - 'lower half of a door, interior door' D1;
    'latticed door' NE2 [OE <u>hæċ</u>] cf. "steek the
    heck", HATCH
heck-berry - 'prunus padus' S2; 'bird-cherry' S3, NE2
    (+**hagberry**) [cf. Dan. <u>hægge-bær</u>]

heckle - 'protective cover e.g. of a fighting-cock' D1; **hackle** 'skin of an ox/cow' e.g. "rough-hackled" D1; 'complexion' NE2 [MidE hechele]

hedgehog - 'a snarl on a rope' N3

heed - see HEAD

heft - 'knife-handle' S2; **haft** 'handle' NE2 [OE hæft]

hell/hail - 'to pour (out)' NE2 Brockett as D'm/N'land; **heald** 'to pour from a pot' D1 Kennet; **helle** 'to pour out' NE1; **hield** 'to tip and pour' D1 [OE hieldan, ON hella]

hellish - 'stylish/daring' E3,W3 {Wright as Yorx/WMids}

hemmel - 'a shed for cattle' D1,NE2,S3; 'a thatched or open shed' E2; **hemble/hemle** 'any place covered overhead and open on both sides' D1; **helm** 'a hovel' NE1 [?OE helm 'protection']

hempy - 'mischievous' NE2,E2 [= ?impish; ?liable to be hanged]

hens than **poultry/chickens**

HER: **hor** T3; **horsell** 'herself' T3

heronsew - 'a heron' S2,NE2 [< Fr heronceau '(small) heron']

hettle - 'hasty' T2; **hetter** 'eager, keen' NE1 [MidE het(t)er]

HEWER: **yewer** E3; cf. **pit-yacker** = hacker; **yew** 'to hew' E3

hike - 'to swing' NE2 (as trans.vb.+**heyk**),T2,T3; **hykin** 'heaving as on the sea' T2

HIMSELF: **hissel** S2,T2; **hessell** T3; **himsel'** T2; cf. **her**

hind - 'farm-bailiff NE2,N2; 'farm-labourer' E2 [MidE hine 'servant' < OE]

hindberries - see RASPBERRIES

hin(d)most - 'last' S2,T2,D1

hinny - 'honey, dearest' T2,NE2,S2,N2,N3,W3,E2 Palgrave (esp. of children); "singin' hinnies"

94

- 'griddle-cakes with currants' T2 {Palgrave
as more Northerly influence} [Brockett
regards as <u>honey</u> in Irish pronunciation]

hing(s) - see HANG

hipe - 'to gore' D1,NE2

hipping - 'a nappy' NE2,E3 [*OED* as in use mid
C18th+]

hissel - see HIMSELF

HIT: pret. **hat** S2,T2 (+**hot**); p.p. **hitten** T2,T3

hit - 'it' T2

hitch - 'to hop' S2,NE2 (+**hip**) [MidE 'to move
jerkily']

hitch - 'a fault in the strata' N2,N3

hiving - 'ivy' S2

hob - 'cooking-range': "as hard as the hobs of Hell"
(E3, of an object, etc.)

hobby - 'child-word for goose' S2; **hoddy** 'the call to
a goose' NE2 [cf. OFr <u>hobet</u> 'a hawk']

hockle - 'phlegm' E3 cf. **cockle**

hoff - see OFTEN

hogg - 'young unshorn sheep' D1,NE2 [see *OED* <u>hog</u>
II.4]

hoggers - 'stockings with feet cut off' T2,NE2,E2
(+'hosepipe'); 'gaiters' T3; 'flannel drawers'
T2; 'miners' work shorts' N3,E3 [source
unknown but with sense of 'stockings' first
recorded C17th, as 'pipe', mid C19th]

by hokey - 'by the devil' N2

hoit - 'slut' e.g. "Ye mucky hoit!" E2; **hoyting** 'riotous
mirth' NE2

HOLD: **ahaad** T3, ?noun; **haad** vb. E2,E3, **ha'd**
T2,NE2, **hod** S2; p.p. **hauden** S2;
[HOLD, cont.]
haud! 'stop' T2; **haud** noun NE2; "haud yor
gob" N2,E3; "haud thee jaw" T2,S2; **hadaway!** 'term of encouragement' NE2, except
in "hadaway ti hell!"; **haudaway** 'get along'
T2; cf. **how**

95

hollin - 'holly' S2 [OE holen]

HOME: **hame** D1,T2; **hyem** T2,N2; **h'yam** S2; **haem**
T2; **yem** N2; **yam** E2,S2,W3 [OE hām]

hoolet - see OWL

hoots! - 'hush!' N2; **hotes** E2; **hout** T1, 'an
exclamation of disapprobation or dissent' T2

hor - see HER

horn-book - 'a child's book' S2 [ABC display with
thin horn covering]

horn-top - 'snail' E2, "as slow as a horntop"

hough - 'the ham or upper joint of the leg' D1;
"cruick thy hough" - 'sit down' NE2,T2; see
also **haughs**

HOURS: **oors** N2

how! - a greeting, NE2 Brockett (+**how-marrow!**);
'hey!' N2,N3,E3; **hae!** 'really!' E2

how-away 'come along!' T2; **how'ay** T2; **howay!**
S2,N2; 'come along' S2; **har away** E2;
haway! E3; **hawoy** 'a call to horses to veer
left' E2; cf. HOLD

howdy - 'the midwife' T2,NE2,E2

howk - 'to make a hole or cut earth with a spade' D1;
'to dig' T2; 'to scoop out a rough hole in the
ground' NE2; 'to dig or scoop out, or punish'
N3; 'to dig or hew out' E2,T2,S3 (+**hoke**),E3;
hoke 'to scoop out' S2; **holkit** 'made a way by
digging or otherwise' D1; **haak** 'to pull' T3;
howk 'to belabour, beat' T3 [cf. OE holc
'cavity' / Swed. halka] var. **yowk** E3

howther - 'rubbish, odds and ends' S2

hoy - 'to throw, heave' NE2,N3,E2,E3; "it's hoying
down it doon whole watter" - 'raining hard'
[**hoy**, cont.]
NE2,E3 [cf.Scot. hoyse, Norw. hissa, but
also Dutch hijschen ?via C17th maritime
contacts; see also *OED* s.v. hoick]

huff'd - 'offended' S2,E3 (+**huff** 'a sulk') [C18th
slang]

hug - 'to carry, manhandle' NE2,N2,S2,S3
gan huggin - to go birdnesting; "to huggies a nest" -
    to rob a nest E3
huildoo - see **yule doo**
humblick - 'hemlock' NE2; "mild as a hum(b)lick" E2
hung on - see HANG
hungered, besides **hungry** NE2
hunkers - 'the hams' T2; 'the buttocks' N3; 'the
    haunches' T2,E2 (+**hench/hinch**); "sitting on
    their hunkers" - 'squatting' NE2,N3 [cf. Du.
    hukken, OFr hanche]
hupstitch - in phrase "every hupstitch" - 'every now
    and again' E2
huse - 'a short cough' D1
huz - see US / **hykin'** - see **hike**

I: **Aw** T2,N2,S2; **Aa** S2,E2,W2,E3,N3,T3; **Aw's** etc. -
    see BE
i' - see IN
ICICLE: **iceshoggle** T2,W2; **iceshockle** S2; **shoggle**
    T2; [cf. Dan. isjokkel]
IN: **i'** N1,T2,S2,N2,S2,S3,W3; **iv** (before vowel;
    Brockett, "so pronounced by country
    people") NE2,T2,S2,E2,S3; **it** N2; **ed** 'in the'
    W2, **id** W2; **intiv** (before vowel) 'into'
    T2,S2,N2,T3
in-bye - 'towards the work-face or interior' N3 etc
ing - 'common pasture, meadow' NE1; **ings** 'low wet
    ground' D1; **ing** 'a meadow' NE2,S3 [ON eng
    'meadow']
inglenook - 'corner by the fire' W2 [?< Gaelic
    aengeal 'fire, light']
insense - 'to inform' NE1; 'to make someone
    understand' NE2,E2,N3
intiv - see IN / **is** - see BE
iron - with 'r' sounded E3
IT: **hit** T2
it/iv - see IN / **ivor** etc., - see EVER

izzard - 'name for the letter "z"' NE2,S2

jack - 'jacket, jerkin' W1 [OFr. jaque]
jackjaw - 'jackdaw' E2
jagger - 'pony' S3; **jagger-galloway** 'a pedlar's pony'
　　　　NE2 [jagger = a carrier, pedlar]
jaistering - 'swaggering' S2,NE2,S3
jallop'd - 'spiked (a drink)' N2 (Barrass, cf. Allan
　　　　p.411); **jollup/jalap** 'the powder of the dried
　　　　tubercles of Exogonium Purga - a purgative'
　　　　T2 [< Jalapa in Mexico]
jannock - 'square, honest behaviour' S2; 'square,
　　　　honest' S3; **jannick** 'staunch, firm' NE2
　　　　Brockett as Yorx; **jenick** 'honest' T2; 'proper,
　　　　right' NE2 [?19th century slang]
jarbled - 'wettened' S2; 'wetted in dew' NE2;
　　　　'bedraggled' S3
jarp - 'to strike eggs together at Easter, in sport'
　　　　NE2,E3
jarsey - 'jersey, type of wool' S2 [< Island of Jersey]
　　　　cf. **Gansey**
jaup - 'to shake any liquid' S2; 'to agitate water etc'
　　　　NE2 [?=jalp, C16th]
jealoused - 'suspected' NE2; 'guessed, anticipated
　　　　(s.thing wd happen)' N3 [OFr gelos]
jee/jye - 'to turn (s.thing) round' (trans.) NE2; cf. **ajee-**
　　　　y
jell - 'piece of wood' E3 [=deal]
jimmer: "a gimmer tree" - 'a tree that grows double
　　　　from the root' D1 Kennet; **jimmers** 'small
　　　　hinges' S2,NE2; 'door hinges' D1; 'pointed
　　　　hinges' NE1 [OFr gemel 'twin']
jimmers - 'ewe sheep, between 1st and 2nd shearing'
　　　　NE2; **gimmer lamb** 'ewe lamb' D1 Kennet as
　　　　Northern; sg. 'rascal' E2 [ON gymbr 'ewe-
　　　　lamb']
jimmy - 'smart, spruce' S2
jinny-howlet - see OWL

jinny-spinner - 'daddy-long-legs' S2,NE2 [?<u>Jeanie</u>
i.e. female]

joinedy-up-writing - 'adult handwriting' E3

joggle - 'to jostle' S2; 'to shake' T2; 'to cause to totter'
NE2; **joggly** 'un-steady' S2; **joley** [sic] T3
[<u>jog</u>, ?C16th vb.] cf.**coggly**

Jonty - 'John' T3,E3

jowl - 'to test for soundness with a stick; to knock, as
a miner's signal' NE2,E2,T3,N3 [see *OED*
<u>jowl</u> sb.4]

jowl - 'lower jaw' S2,NE2; 'flesh on a pig's jaw' E2;
also a threat as "A'l jowl tha" E2,N3 [OE
<u>ċeolor</u> 'cheek']

jud - 'coal-face ready for taking down' T2,NE2,N2,E2
[see *OED* s.v. <u>jud</u>, <u>jad</u>]

jumly - 'muddy' (water) E2

junters - 'sulky, peevish' S2

ka! - a signal in driving cattle N1; 'give over!' T2;
kar! NE2 Brockett as Newc.

kaingey - see **caingy**

kale - 'cabbage, greens' NE2; 'coleworts' D1; **kail**-pot
'pot for cooking cabbage, stew etc' NE2,S2,E2
[ON <u>kál</u>]

kanches - see **canches**

katty-keys - 'ash-tree seeds' S2

keek - 'to peep' T2 Wilson ('slily'),NE2; 'look' T3;
keeker 'an overlooker, foreman' NE2,T2,E2;
'surface foreman' N3 [ON <u>kįkja</u> 'to pry'; cf.
Du. <u>kijken</u>]

keel - 'coal-barge' NE2; 'a large cargo boat' T3 [OE
<u>ceol</u> 'boat']

kellick - 'unfledged bird' E2; **raw kellick** E3; "a new
kelk" NE2 Brockett as Durham

kelk - 'a blow' NE2,S3, S2 Dinsdale (+'a small
species of hemlock'); 'the ordinary field
hemlock' NE2 [re plant see *OED* **kex/keck**]

kelter - 'money' NE2,T2,S2; 'riches' T2;
kelterman/kelterment 'odds & ends, scrap'
E3, 'rubbish' S3

kemping - 'competitive hand-reaping' D1; **cample** 'to
argue back' NE2 [OE cempa 'competitor',
MidE kemping 'football']

ken - 'to know, discern' D1,T2,S2,N2,E2; pret.
kend/kent S2,E2; "dinna ken" E2 Palgrave as
Bihsop Auckland [OE cennan, ON kenna]
cf. KNOW

kenner - 'the end of the shift' N3; **kennor** N2; 'time
to cease work' E2

kenspecked - 'marked or branded' NE1 Ray; 'markt
or branded with spots or speckles' D1
Kennet as Northern; **kenspeckled**
'particularly marked so as to be easily
known' NE2 Brockett; 'of distinctive
appearance' S2; **kenspeckle** 'noted' T2;
kenspreckled 'well-known, marked' E2 [cf.
Norw. kjennespak 'quick to spot (s.thing)']
cf. **spreckled**

kep - 'to catch' S2,NE2,N3,T2,T3; "to kep a ball" NE1
[OE cēpan 'to seize, keep']

kerve - see **kirve**

keslop - 'calf rennet' D1,NE2 Brockett (+'stomach')
[OE cȳslybb 'cheese-chemical']

kessen - p.p. 'cast' T2, "the weather's owerkessen"
S3; **cassen** 'cast off' T2, 'fallen over' (of ewe)
W3(C'land); **kest** 'to throw away' S2 (+p.p.
kast) [=cast, ON kasta]

ket - 'poor (meat)' T2, 'filth or rubbish' NE2,N3,S3,
'anything inedible' E2, 'offal,filth,carrion' S2;
[**ket**, cont.]
ketty 'worthless' NE2,S2; **kets** 'sweets' W3,E3
[?< ON kiöt 'flesh' > 'sweetmeats'?]

kevel - 'a great lout or heavie ffellow' D1 Kennet
(+**kafil**); 'large hammer in a stone-quarry' D1

Bailey,S2 [?< ON <u>kefli</u> 'a stick'; cf. Scot <u>kyvel</u> 'to hammer']

kibble - 'large iron bucket used for raising material up and down shaft in a mine' E2,N3; 'small low tub with open end' N3; 'tippable coal-tub' E3; **kivil** 'vehicle for stone' E3; **kimmel** 'a poudring tub' NE1 [Ger. <u>kübel</u> 'tub']

kicky-can - 'kid's game' E3

kilter: "out of kilter" - 'out of sorts, condition' E3

kink - 'to breathe or laugh in spasms' NE2; **king-cough** 'whooping cough' NE1,S2 [OE <u>ċincung</u> 'heavy laughter']

kirk - see CHURCH / **kirn** - see CHURN / **kirsen** - see CHRISTEN / **Kirsmas** - see CHRISTMAS

kirve - 'to undercut coal prior to blasting' T2, **curve** N2; **kerve** 'to cut, carve' D1 [=carve < OE <u>ċeorfan</u> + ch>k)]

kist - 'a chest' D1,NE2,T2,E2,S2 (+chist); **chist** S2; "deputy's kist" N3,E3 [OE <u>ċist</u>, ON <u>kista</u>]

kit - 'a milking pail with 2 ears and a cover' NE1; 'a small washing tub' E2,S2; 'small pail' NE2 [cf.MidDu. <u>kitte</u>]

kite - 'belly' D1 Ray as C'land, D1,E2,T3; **kyte** S2; 'a belly or womb' D1 Kennet as Northern; **howl-kite** 'empty stomach' T2 [cf. Du. <u>kijte</u> 'any fleshy part of body']

kittle - 'to tickle' D1,NE2,S2,T2,T3; "kittle the fire" E3; adj. 'uncertain, doubtful' NE1; 'ticklish, difficult' T2,E2,NE2, **kittlish** S2 [ON <u>kitla</u>, MidDu. <u>kitelen</u>]

kittlin' - 'a young cat' T2 Robson (+'tickling'); **kitten** E2; **kittlen** T2

kitty - 'house of correction' NE2; 'lock-up' T2,E2 [? after Kidcote jail]

kissen'd - see **guizen**

knack/nack - 'to speak finely or affect a fine soft pronunciation (applied to those who speak in the southern dialect)' D1 Kennet as

Northern,NE1,NE2; **knacked** 'finished,
worn-out' E3; **knack-kneed** 'knock-kneed'
NE2 (+**knacky-kneed**); [=knock; cf. Du.
knakken]
knap - 'a blow' S2,NE2; **naup** 'to strike as
punishment' S2 [cf. Dan. knep]
KNOW: **knaw** S2,T2,NE2,N2 (**naw**),S2,E3 etc;
knawn (p.p.) S2,T2; neg. **dináa** 'don't know'
E2,E3 [MidEN knawen (p.p.) < OE cnāwen]
cf. **ken**
knowled - see **noll**
kodd - see CUSHION / **kye** - see COWS

labber - 'to dabble in water' S2; **labbering**
'floundering' NE2
lace - 'to lash, thrash' S2,NE2,T3 [OFr. lacier]
lad than boy E2
lade (**l'yad**) - 'to load' S3; noun 'a load' NE2
the lafe - 'the residue or all that is left' D1 Kennet;
lave D1 Ray as C'land, NE2 [OE lāf + ON
læifr]
laggans - 'staves of a tub' E2 [ON logg]; "black
laggie" - 'wooden dish with handle, for
children' D2
lake - 'to play' NE1,D1,NE2,S2,W2; 'to play or lark'
S3; **laker** 'a player' NE2; **lakes** 'sports, games'
S2; **babby-lakin** 'child's toy' S2,NE2; **laikins**
'toys' (C'land); **play-lakin** 'a simpleton' E2
[ON læika, OE lācan]
lames - 'injuries' E3 e.g. "he got his lames" [cf. OE
lambyrd 'lame- i.e. mis-birth']
lang - 'long' S2,T2,W2,S2 etc. [OE lang]
lap - 'to wrap' S2,E2 [cf. Du. lappen]
lap - see also LOWP
LAPWING: **tufit** S3 [*OED* s.v. tewhit]; **peesweep**
'lapwing or peewit' E2; **pee-wit** or **peez-weep**
NE2; "pee-wit land" - 'cold, wet, badland,

102

which the peewit generally haunts' NE2
[onom.]

lass than <u>girl</u> S2,E2; **lassie** S2,T3 [presumed ON
<u>lasqa</u> 'unmarried']

latch - 'to alight properly, as "a cat latchath upon her
feet"' D1 Kennet [OE lǣċan]

late - 'to seek' NE1,D1; 'to search' S2; **late/leat** 'to
search, seek, summon' NE2; **lait** S3 [ON
<u>leita</u>]

lathered - 'hot and sweaty' E3

leach - 'hard-work, great fatigue, a word frequent
among the miners in the north' D1 Kennet

lead - 'to carry, convey' S2,NE2,E2

leam - 'a flame' D1,NE2 [OE <u>lēoma</u>]

learn - 'to teach' S2,E2; **larn** T3; **lairn** 'to learn'
S2,T2; **unlarn'd** 'unlearned' T2 [OE
<u>leornian</u>]

leazes - 'gently sloping fields' S2; 'common pasture'
NE2 [OE <u>lǣswe/lǣs</u>]

lee (noun/vb.) 'lie, fib' S2,T2,NE2,T2,S2; **lee-ar** 'liar'
S2,T2

leet (on) - 'to light upon, come across' S2,NE2,W2;
let 'alighted' T3; **leet** 'a light' T2,N2; **leet-ship**
'unloaded ship' T2; **leets** 'animal lungs' S2

lemurs - 'ripe nuts easily unhusked' D1; **leemer** S2;
leam 'ripe hazel-nut' NE2 [*OED* s.v.
<u>leam(er)</u>]

LET: "let wi't" - 'let on' S2; p.p. **letten** T3

letch - 'a marshy gutter or swampy ground' D1; **leche
or leak** 'a gutter' D1; 'a wet ditch' NE2; **leck**
'to leak' S2 [OE <u>leccan</u> 'to wetten']

lib - 'to castrate' NE1,D1,S2,NE2 [OE <u>lyb</u> 'drug,
medicine'; Du. <u>lubben</u> 'to geld' and cf. Scot.
<u>libbet</u> 'castrated']

library - 'a library book' E2,E3

lick - 'to beat, chastise' S2,W2; 'to beat, overcome'
N2; **licks** 'punishment' NE2,S2; **fullick** 'a
forceful blow' N3 [?C16th slang]

lief - 'rather' D1,NE2; **lieve** 'willingly' S2,NE2; **liever**
    D1 Kennet as N'land [OE lēof, 'dear']
lig - 'to lie (down)' NE1,D1,NE2 [ON liggja; cf. N.
    lee/lie < OE licgan]
lignies - 'wooden quoits; last few marbles' E2;
    liggee/lignie 'quoit' NE2; **ligny** 'knor or ball
    for spell & knor' S2; **liggies** 'marbles' E3,
    'testicles' N3 [< lignum vitae]
likeness than photo S3
limbers - 'shafts of a carriage' E2; **limmers**
    S2,NE2,N3 [?Fr. limon]
limmer - 'rascally, delinquent' W1; 'a rogue' NE2;
ling - 'common heath plant' NE1,D1,S2,W2p,S2 [ON
    lyng]
lingey - 'limber' NE1; 'strong, active, with endurance'
    D1; **linjy** S2 [OFr. ligne/linge]
linn - 'a cascade' D1,W2,NE2 Brockett as D'm/N'land
    [OE hlynn, Welsh llyn]
linty - 'wren' T3; 'linnet' T2; **linty** 'white linnet' NE2;
    lennet 'linnet' S2
lippen (on) - 'to depend, rely' (on s.one to do s.thing)
    D1 Ray as Scots,E2; 'depend on' T2,NE2;
    lippen to (C'land)
lish - 'nimble, active' NE2,S3; 'strong, sturdy' e.g. of a
    man T2; **lisk** S2; **leesh** 'active, supple' T2
lisk - 'that part of the side which is between the hips
    and the short ribs' D1 Kennet as Yorx; 'groin'
    S2,NE2; 'thigh' E2 [cf. Dan. lyske, OE lesca]
list - 'desire, energy' E2; **unlisty** 'listless' T2 [OE
    lystan (vb), ON lysta; cf. Ice. lyst 'appetite']
lithe - 'to listen' D1,NE2 [ON hlyða]
lithe - 'to thicken' (s.thing) S2, NE2
LEACH: **loach** D1 Bailey
lock - 'small amount' e.g. of meal S2; "a loke sand"
    NE2 [?Fr. loque]
logger-head - 'a coloured butterfly, large moth' E2

lonning - 'a lane' E2; **lonnin** N1,S2,T2,S2, **lonnen**
W2; **loaning/lonnin** 'lane or bye-road' NE2;
back-lon E2 [old variant of lane]

looka! - 'see here' E3; **lucka!** T2; **looks-tha** 'an
expression to gain attention' E2

look - see **luke**

lop - 'a flea' D1 Kennet as Yorx, NE2,S2,T2,E2,E3;
loppy 'itchy' E3 [O.Dan. loppe]

loppit - 'sour or curd milk' E2; "loppered milk"
NE2,T2 [ON hloypa 'to curdle']

lork!/lowk! - 'Lord!' N2; **lawk!** S2

loss than lose e.g."to loss s.thing"; p.p. "Aa've loss
that" E3

lot - in "a lot way, a lot brass" etc.; **lorra** 'lot of' E3
[cf. **bit**]

lough - 'a pond or standing pool' D1,NE2 [Gaelic,
loch]

lowe - 'the flame of a fire' D1,S2; 'light or flame'
T2,NE2,N3; 'a flame'
NE1,D1,T2,S2,N2,E2,T3; "gis a low" - 'give
me a light' N3; **alow** 'alight' (of a cigarette)
T3; vb. 'to flame' as "the fire lows" D1 Kennet
as Yorx [MidEN low, ON logi]

lownd - 'sheltered' S2; **lound** 'calm' (day) S2 [cf. Ice.
lugn 'calm']

lowp - 'to leap, jump' etc D1,NE2,T2 Wilson
(**loup**),E2,E3 (esp.**lowpin**'), T3; **lope** NE1,S2
(+noun); pret. **lap** T2,NE2,S2,T2; **lop** E3;
lowpt N2,S2 [ON hlaupa]

lowse - 'to loosen' T2,N2,E3 (e.g."lowse haad ovit");
louse NE2 Brockett; **louze** S2; **lowse** 'to
finish work' S2,NE2,E2; adj. T2 [ON lauss
(adj. 'free')]

luke - 'to weed' D1; **look** 'to weed corn' S2; **lowk**
NE1; **looking** 'weeding' NE2 Brockett esp. of
corn [OE ālūcan + ON lúka; see OED s.v.
louk]

lug - 'the ear' D1,NE1,T2,S2,NE2,E2,S2,E3; vb. 'to
carry' S2,S3 [ON <u>lugg</u> 'a handle, something
to pull']
lum - 'chimney' E2; "a loom or lumm" - 'a chimney'
D1 [Welsh <u>llumon</u> or OFr <u>lum</u> 'light']

Ma - see MOTHER
maddle - 'to forget, be confused' NE2,S2; 'to be fond
of' D1, NE1 [<<u>mad</u>]
maffle - 'To be perplexed, fail' NE2 [cf. Du. <u>maffelen</u>
'to mouth']
mafted - 'tired, knocked back, overcome' S3; **maftin**'
'stifling' S3
MAGPIE: **maggie** NE2,S3; **maggies** 'Newcastle Utd
supporters' E3; **piat/piannet** 'magpie' S2
Dinsdale (where 1=sorrow, 2=luck, 3=a
wedding, 4=a death); **pyet** D2
maister 'master, boss' S2,T2,NE2; 'mine-owner' N2
MAKE: **maek** T2; **myek** T2,N2; **mak**
NE2,S2,W2,E2,S2; "maks nae odds" E3;
pres.p. **mekken**' W3; pret. **m'yed** NE2, **m'yad**
S2; "makkums an' takkums" Sunderland folk
(as manufacturers); {**mak** esp. Durham &
Yorx, **mek** in N'land; also **myek** found}
mal - 'to dress carelessly' D1
mal (pron. <u>maal</u>) - 'rubble-built wall' E2
malkin' NE2 'a dirty wench', **maelin**' T2 [?< dimin.
form of <u>Maud</u>]
Mally - 'Mary' T2; 'a hare' NE2 Brockett as Durham
MAN: **mon** - 'man!' - of anyone E2,S2,etc. **mun** T2
[OE <u>monn</u> '(any) person']
man - see also MUST / **mang** - see amang
mang - 'wholemeal barley, oats as animal feed' D1;
'oats ground with husks' NE2,S3; 'a mash of
bran' S2 [< OE ġemang 'mixture']
marrow - 'a fellow or companion, and the relative
term in pairs' D1,NE1; 'a matched pair'
S2,NE2; 'partner, companion' T2,E2; 'an

equal, comrade' T2,NE2, **marra** E2; **marra**
'workmate' N2,N3; 'friend' E3,G3 {now only
D'm,N'land,C'land} [ON <u>margr</u> 'friendly']
mash (S) / **mask** (N) - 'to mash or brew tea';
    mast/mash E3; **mast** T3; **mask** NE2; [Dan.
    <u>maske</u>]
maslin - 'flour or bread made of mixed grains' NE2
    (+**masselgem**) [OE <u>mæstling</u> / OFr
    <u>mestreillon</u>]
matterless - 'immaterial, of no importance' E2
maugh - 'a brother-in-law' D1; **meaugh** 'my wives
    brother or sisters husband' NE1;
    maugh/mauf/meaugh NE2; **maug/meaugh** 'a
    wife's brother' D1 [ON <u>mágr</u>]
maumy - 'mellow and juiceless' D1; 'mellow' S2;
    mome 'soft, smooth, sweet' NE2 [see OED
    s.v. <u>malmy</u>]
maundering - 'listless, idle' S2; to maunder 'to be
    vague in action or thought' NE2
mawks - 'maggots' D1 Kennet as Yorx,
    T2,NE2,S2,S3, **mauks** NE1; **mawky** 'rotten'
    S3 (+**mawked**) [MidE <u>maðek</u>, ON <u>maðkr</u>]
MAYBE: **mevies** - 'perhaps' T2,N2,T3; **mavies** NE2;
    mebbe T2,S2,NE2,S2,E2,N2 (+**mebbies**)
mazed - 'bewildered' S2,NE2 [late OE <u>āmasod</u>, cf.
    Norw. <u>masa</u> 'to toil, worry']
ME: **mah** W2; **ma** S2; see also MY
meat - 'any food' E2 [OE <u>mete</u>, '(solid) food']
meg - 'halfpenny' T3; "Aa hevnt got a meg" E3 [<u>mag</u>,
    late C18th term]
meg - 'to spit' e.g. "he's megging' at us" S3
mell - 'a wooden sledge or beatle' D1,T2,S2; 'a mallet
    or beetle' NE1; 'wooden hammer with long
    handle' S2,NE2; 'large wood or iron hammer'
    N3,E3,T3 [Fr. <u>mail</u>]
mell with - 'to meddle (with)' D1,S2,NE2 [Fr. <u>mêler</u>]
mel-supper - 'harvest-home celebration' D1,NE2
    [ON <u>mele</u>, 'corn']

mense - 'good manners' D1 Kennet as N'land;
'politeness, consideration' E2; 'propriety'
NE2; vb. 'to grace, decorate, show respect to'
T1,T2,NE2; **menseful** 'comely, graceful'
NE1,D1; 'polite, hospitable' S2,E2,NE2 [ON
mennska 'proper conduct']

merle - 'blackbird' S3 {in use in Scot/Ire} [<Fr]

messet - 'an ill-bred dog' T2; 'small dog e.g. spaniel'
S2; 'a small dog, a sort of cur' NE2 (+**messan**)
[Scot. messan <Gael. measan]

mickle - 'much' D1,NE1,S2,T2; 'much, big' NE2
Brockett as D'm/ N'land,E2 Palgrave as rare;
mich, mitch S2 [MidEN mikel, OE micel,
ON mikla]

midding - 'a dunghill' NE1; 'a maxen or dunghill' D1;
'dung-heap' T2; **middin** 'earth-toilet' S2; **dry
midden** E3, as out-of-date; **midden-crow** 'the
carrion crow' NE2; **midden-cart** 'dung-cart'
E2, 'dust-cart' E3 [ON mykidyngja]

midgies - 'gnats' NE1,D1,S2,NE2,N2 [OE mycg];
midgey 'open lantern used in mine' E2,N3
[Brockett as <midge's ee]

mind - 'to remember' S2,NE2,E2,T3; 'remind,
remember' T2; **ming** 'to mind or observe...';
minging, 'a mentioning or putting in mind'
D1,NE2 [OE myndgian]

mint - 'fantastic, champion' E3

mizzle - 'slight rain' S2,NE2,T3; vb. NE2,S3 [cf. Du.
miezelen]

mizzle off - 'go away' N2,N3 [late C18th term]

mizzy - 'a quagmire' NE1,D1 [MidE misy ?< OE
mēos, 'moss']

MOLE: **mold-warp** D1 Kennet as Yorx; **moudiwarp**
D1,NE2,S2 (cf.Scot. **moudiewart**);
mou(l)diwarp/moudie T3 [<MidE = 'earth-
turner']; **moley-rat** E2; **mowdy-rat** NE2,E3;
moudiheap 'molehill' S3; **want** 'a mole' NE2
Brockett as Northern) [see *OED* want sb.1,

108

where traced to MidE <u>want</u>, OE <u>wond</u>, cf OE
<u>wendan</u> 'to turn'. However *OED* claims <u>want</u>
for 'mole' is "unknown" in the Northern
counties.]

monifeet - 'centipede' S2; **meg-monny-feet**
    '?millipede' NE2

moor-hen - 'red grouse' W1

MORE: **mair** T2,S2,N2,E3,T3; **mare** S2,W2; **maist**
    'most' S2,NE2

MOTHER: **Ma** E2; **Mammy** NE2,T2,S2 (+**Mam**),W3;
    Mudder S2; **Minny** T2; **Nanna** 'grand-
    mother' E3; **Ganny** E3

mow - 'to stack corn in a barn' S2 (pron.<u>moo</u>);
    "mow'd off" - 'packed full' E3. pron. <u>maoo</u>-;
    [OE <u>mūga</u> + ON <u>muge</u> 'a stack of hay']; **mow**
    'to have intercourse with a woman' D1,S2

mud - see MUST

mugger - 'tinker, itinerant pot-seller' N2,N3 [from
    <u>mug</u>, item of saleable earthenware]

muggles - 'a game of marbles' S3, "play muggles"E3

mun - see MUST

murl - 'to crumble away' S2 [?<OE <u>mearu</u> 'soft']

MUST: pres. **mun/man** D1 Kennet as Yorx,
    NE2,T2,S2,N2; **munnet** 'must not' T2,
    munnot NE2,S2, **mooant** S2, **maunit/munnit**
    T2; "they mustn't be making much money" =
    'can't..' E3; pret. **mud** S2 (+**mighted**) {most
    D'm = **munnot**; N/T **mustn't**, Cleve. **maun't**}
    [ON <u>mun</u>]

muthy - 'close' (of weather) S3

MY: **maw** T2,NE2,S2,N2; **mah** W2,S2 (+**me**); **me**
    N2,W2, **mi** W2,W3; **mesel** 'myself' S2;
    mysel'/mawsel T2, **mysell** S2,T2

naack/nae - see NO

nab - 'abrupt termination of hilly ridge' S2,NE2
    Brockett re D'm place-names {also C'land}
    [<ON <u>nabbr</u>] cf. **neb**

nack - see **knack** / **naen** - see NONE

nantle - 'to do s.thing in an easy and careless
      manner' S2

naup - see **knap**

neaf/naife pl. **neaves** - 'a hand or fist' D1;
      neive/neiffe 'a fist' NE1; **neive** 'the fist' D1,
      neeve T2, **nief** NE2, **neif/neaf** S2; **neif** 'hand'
      E2; **double-neif** 'clenched fist' E2,NE2 [ON
      hnefi 'fist'] cf. **neivel**

neat - sg. 'ox, bullock' etc; as collective noun, 'cattle'
      D1 [OE nēat] cf. **nowt**

neb - 'bill of a bird, point of a pen etc.' NE1; 'bill,
      beak' S2,NE2,T2; 'nose' T3,S3; **nebs** 'mouths'
      T2; **nebby** 'nosey' E3 [OE nebb] cf. **nab**

nedder - 'an adder' NE2 Brockett as N'land, T3 [OE
      nǣdre]

Neeb - 'Northern Electricity Board' E3

neeze - 'sneeze' S2 [ON hnjósa - and so a valid form]

NEITHER: **neether** N2; **nowther** T2,S2,NE2,S2
      (+**nowder**)

neivel - 'to strike with the fist' D1; **nevel** S2,NE2;
      neifle/nevel S3 [< **neaf**]

nenst - see **anenst**

nesh - 'soft, tender' NE1,D1 [OE hnesce]

netty - 'toilet' E3 (+lavvy),T3 {D'm, N'land only}
      [C18th nessy (necessary) ?+ Italian/WWI
      cabinetti)

neuled - see **noll**

NEVER: **nivver/nivor** S2,W2,N2, **niver** T2; **nivor**
      prefered to not

nevvy - 'nephew'E2

neway - 'nowhere' T2; 'no way' E3

nick - 'to cut' (esp. sides of jud, at coal-face) T2,NE2;
      nick-stick 'a tally stick' NE2,W2; **nick-nacks**
      'trifles' T2

nicker - 'to neigh, laugh' T2,NE2; "nickering and
      hockering" - 'sniggering and laughing' S3
      [onom.]

niere - see **ear**

NIGHT: **neet** D1,S2,T2,NE2,W2; **neit** T1; pron. nait
E3, but for **badger-neet** 'Friday night'

nip than pinch NE1,S2

nithered - 'frozen' E3 [?OE niðerian 'to bring down']

NOBODY: **nee-body** 'nobody, no one' W2

nobbut - see BUT

noll - 'to strike' E2; **nell-kneed** 'knock-kneed' T2;
"knowled down" - 'kept under the thumb' E3;
"neuled down" - 'weighed down' S3 [see
OED s.v. knell]

NO: **nay/ne** (adj.) N2, **nae/nee** T1,T2
(+**ne/na**),E2,E3,T3,N3; **na** S2; **neea** S2; **naw**
(emphatic) + **na** (unstressed) T2,T3; **ne** T2;
adv.; **na** T2,S2,E3,T3; **naack** 'no' T3 {Scot.
nae = no, na = not} [MidEN na, OE nā]

NONE: **naen** T2, **n'yan** S2; **nyen** T2,N2; **naane** W2;
neean S2 [OE nān]; **neean** 'no one' E3 cf.
NOBODY

NOOK: **neauk** D1; **neuk/nuick** 'chimney-nook' T2
[MidE; cf. Norw. nók 'hook, something bent']

nor prefered to than (after comparison) NE1,E2

NOT: **nut** T2,S2,W2,S2

NOUGHT: **nowt/nowse** - 'nothing' T2,NE2; **nowt**
S2,T2,N2,W2,T3,E2; "a 9 with the tail cut
off" - 'a useless person' E3; **half-nowt** 'half-
price' T2 [OE nāht]

nows and thens - 'now and then' E2

nowt - see NOUGHT

nowt - 'cattle' S2 e.g. "Darlington Nowt Fair";
nolt/nout D1, NE2 [ON naut] cf. **neat**

OAK: **aik** D1,S2 (+**yak**); **yak** D1,S2; **yek** NE2 [OE āc]

OF: **o'** T2,N2,E2,S2; **a'** N2; **uv** W2; **on't** 'of it' T2

oftens - 'often' E2; **oftens/offens** S2,T2 [explained by
Brockett as the plural of often]; **ofter** 'more
frequently' S2; **hoff** 'often' E2

oky/weaky - 'moist, sappy' D1; **woky** NE2

OLD: **awd** T2; **aud** N2,S2,T2; **aad/owld** T3 [MidEN
ald, OE eald]; **aud-farrant** - see **farand**
ome - 'the smoak, reek, stith or vapour of hot liquids
is called Ome, as the Ome of salt pans' D1
Kennet
ONCE: **yance** D1,NE1,S2; **yence** T2; **yance/ance** D1
ONE: **ane** W1, D1 (**+yan**),S2 (**+yan,yah**); **yan**
D1,S2,W2,NE2,S2 (**+yah**); **yane** NE1; **yen** T2;
un T2; pron. won E2p,E3,etc.; **a one** 'one'
(pronoun) E2,E3; **yan-sell** 'oneself' S2
[MidEN ane, OE ān]
ONLY: **oney** T2,E3
ony - 'any' T2,S2,NE2,N2,E2,W3, etc; **oney** T2; **onny**
S2; **ony body** T2
ool - see OWL / **oor** - see OUR
OR: **er** W2,S2
other - 'another' E2; "the tother" T2, "the tuther" N2
oumar - 'shadow' D1 Kennet as N'land; 'the shade'
NE2; "i't'oomor/owmer" (C'land) [OFr
umbre]
OUR: **wor** T2,E2,T3, **wur** S2,NE2; **oor** (e.g. of a
member of the family) E2,W2
outbye - 'towards the shaft underground' T2,N2;
'out-of-the-way/towards the shaft' E2
Palgrave; **oot-bye** 'outside' T3, 'a short way
from home' NE2
OVEN: **yuvven** T2; **yoon** NE1
ower - 'over' T2,S2,NE2,W1 (**o'er**),W2,W3,E3,T3,N3;
as prefix = 'too' e.g. **ower-big** E2,E3
[**ower**, cont.]
[MidEN ower/oure, our-farr etc.; OE ofer] cf.
give (ower)
OWL: **ool** T2; **hoolet** T2; **hewlet** S2; **ewlet** S3; **howlet**
NE2; **jinny-howlet** 'owl' S2 [?< Jeanie i.e.
female]
OWN: see **awn**
owse - see **owt**/OXEN

owt - 'anything' T2,NE2 (**+ought**),N2,E3,T3; **owght**
W2; **owse** T2 [OE āuht]
OXEN: **owsen** NE2 (**+ousen**); **ousen** NE1,S2 [var. of
oxen]
oxo - 'noughts & crosses' E3
oxter - 'armpit' S2,NE2,E2; **oxtar** D1; "oxter pocket" -
'inside coat pocket' W2 [OE ōxta/ōhsta]

Pace day - 'Easter-day' D1; **Paste-eggs** 'decorated
Easter eggs' NE2,E2 [OFr Pasche 'Easter']
paddock - see TOAD
panker - 'large marble' E2, **penker** T3 {Wright as
D'm only, 'large marble of stone or iron'}
parlish - 'dangerous' S2,NE2; 'remarkable' (C'land)
[<perilous]
part of, than some of E3
PARTRIDGE: **partrick** S3, **paitrich** NE2 [cf.Scot.
pairtrick]
pash - 'a heavy fall of rain' NE2 [cf. Swed. paska 'to
rain heavily'] see also **thunner-pash**
pate - see BADGER
paut - 'to finger or paw' (ground or person) S3; **pout**
'to kick' NE2; 'a punch' (tool) D1; **pouk** 'to
strike or poke' NE2 [var. of poke?]
pawkey - 'particular' T2; 'dainty' E2; **pauky** 'of a
child hard to please' S2 [?< pawk 'a trick']
pay - 'to beat' e.g. a jacket S2; 'to beat, to drub' NE2;
p.p. **paid** 'beaten, over-come' W1
paze - 'to raise, to force open' NE2; 'to lever up' S3
[<OFr, see *OED* s.v. peise]
pea-jacket - 'outer holiday dress of a keelman' T2;
pee 'short jacket' T2 [?Du.]
peedee (P.D.)- 'keelboy' T2; 'young lad in a keel' T2;
'boat's boy' T3; 'anything small' E2,E3 ['foot
servant', C17th]
peesweep - see LAPWING
pick-dark - 'pitch-dark' S3; **pick-night** NE2
piffolo - 'piccolo' E2

113

pit than <u>mine</u> E2; **pitman** T1,E2 (+**pittie**), etc. [OE <u>pytt</u>, 'pit, hole']; **pit-yacker** 'miner' E3, as uncomplimentary [?<<u>hacker</u>, cf. Northumb. <u>hagger</u> 'hewer']; **pitmatic** 'Durham work dialect' E3

pitch-an'-toss - 'game of chance with pennies esp. old cartwheel-pennies' E3; 'quoit-like game' T3

pittle - 'to pee' T3,E3 [=<u>piddle</u>]

pitt'rin' on - 'complaining, whingeing' E2

plack - 'a small coin' T2 [C15th Flemish <u>placke</u>]

planting - 'a plantation' (of trees) E2,E3; **plantation** also common, for managed woodland, E3

plash - 'to splash' D1,NE2; "to plash in the dirt" D1; "plashes doon" - 'pours down' T3; **plashy** 'wet under foot' D1 [cf. Swed. <u>plaska</u> 'to splash'] cf. **blashey**

play-lakin' - see **lake**

plodge - 'to wade' T2,NE2,E2,E3,T3 [var. of <u>plod</u>]

plote - 'to pluck' S2,E3,T3,S3 (**ploat**); 'to pluck or bring down' N3; **plottin'** D2 [cf. Du. <u>ploten</u>]

pluff - 'to spit' T3; 'to blow in the face, to explode gunpowder' NE2; **pluffer** 'peashooter' E3 [cf. Du. <u>ploffen</u> 'to puff, explode']

plukes - 'pimples' T2; **sheep-pluke** W2 [OED <u>plouk</u> <Gaelic <u>pluc</u>]

poke - 'a bag or sack' D1,NE1,S2,NE2,N2,E2 [ON <u>poki</u> 'pouch' cf. OE <u>pocca</u>/<u>pohha</u>] cf. **bate-poke**

póllis - 'police' T2,E2,S2,T3; **a pollis** T2,E3; **pollis-points** 'traffic lights' T3

poss - 'to wash clothes by agitating them in a tub with a stick or <u>dolly</u>' NE2,E2,S2,T3; **posh** 'to stir up (a fire)' S2 [?Fr <u>pousser</u>]

pot than <u>mug</u> (of coffee, etc.) E3 (esp.pits)

POTATO: **tatie** S2,T2; **tettie** T3; **chatties** E3,W3; **taty-garth** 'field of potatoes' E2,E3 as Yorx

priest - 'any clergyman' E2

prod - 'a goad' D1,E3; 'a prick or skewer' NE2;
proddy-mat W3 - cf. next entry
proggle - 'a thorn' E2; **proggles** 'thistles' E3; **to prog**
'action of making a rag-mat' E3; 'to prick'/'a
prickle' NE2,T3; **progley** 'prickly' N3;
proggy-mat 'rug made of strips of old
material' E3 [?=prod]
pross - 'to gossip' NE2,S3; [?=prose]
pubble - 'plump, full' (grain on stem etc.)
NE1,D1,NE2 as C'land [cf. Du. pumpel]
puke than 'vomit' S3; cf. **spew**
pump - 'to fart' E3
punne - 'to pound or beat in a mortar' D1
putte - 'to push with head or horns as a cow' D1
Kennet as Yorx; **to put** 'to push, propel' e.g.
"putting a keel" NE2; 'to push a coal-tub'
T2,N1,E2 etc.
pyker - 'small (herring) boat' D1 [*OED* piker
?<Picardy]

qu- see also **wh-**
queens - 'women' N2 {also Scot.}; **quean** 'a drab, a
slut, a base woman' D1 Kennet (but without
specifying area); **queen-cat** 'she-cat' S2,W;
queenie & **carl-cat** M/F E3; **wheen-cat** & **carl-
cat** NE1; "queen's heads" 'postage stamps'
W2 [OE cwene, 'woman/queen'; ON karl 'a
man']

racken-crouk - 'pot-hanger' D1; **recking-crook** 'hook
for pans to hang on over fire' E2; **ratten-
crouk** NE2; **reckans** NE1 [OE racente + ON
rakendr, 'chain' see *OED* s.v. rackan-crook]
raff - 'spoil, plunder' D1; **raff-yard** 'timberyard' S2,
'scrapyard' T3 [cf. Swed. rafs 'rubbish', Gm.
Raf 'beam of wood']
rageous - 'in a rage' NE2; 'outrageous, violent' E2
raggy - 'stony, of shale' N2 [MidE rag 'stone']

rainbird - '(green) woodpecker' NE2,D2 ["said to be vociferous when rain is impending" *OED*]

ram 'acidic, pungent' S2;'rancid' S3; **ram/rammish** 'foetid' NE2 [cf.Ice.rammr]

rame - 'to weep or cry' D1; 'presistently cry or ask' NE2; 'to ply with questions, nag' E2; **r'yam** 'cry for, persistently' S2; **ream** 'shout very loudly' S2 [ON hreimr 'a scream/cry']

rammel - 'stone that gets mixed with the coal' N3; **rummle** 'rubble' E2 [OFr ramaille 'brushwood, rubbish']

rang - see WRONG

range - 'to rinse' E2; **range/rench** NE2; cf. **rensh**

RASPBERRY: **rasp** S2,NE2,E2; **hindberries** NE1,D1,NE2 [OE hindbrēr 'raspberry bush']

ratherlings - 'for the most part' NE2 Brockett as D'm/N'land

ratten - 'rat' T2,S2,T2,NE2 [MidE ratton]

rattle-scawp - 'mischievous fellow' E2

raw - 'row' i.e. terrace, S2,T2,NE2 etc.

rax - 'to stretch (tight)' T2,S2 (of oneself), NE2,E2,E3 (of gloves); **rack** 'to reach' T2 (+**reech**) [OE raxan]

ream - see CREAM

reckling - 'the weak pig in a litter' E2,E3; **remlin** 'a remnant' S2

red - 'to tidy' e.g. hair S2; 'to put in order' NE2 Brockett (+ D'm variant, **reet** i.e.'right'); 'to ready' esp. "redding s.thing" S3 [MidE red]

reed - 'red' T1,S2,NE2,T3 [MidEN reede, OE rēad]

reek - "in the North they pronounce it 'reek' and use it indifferently for all sort of smoak" De Kennet; 'smoke' E2,S2,W2,T3; vb. 'to smoke' T2,S2,NE2; **powder-reek** i.e. smoke N3 [OE rec, ON reykr]

reesty - 'rusty' (of overripe bacon) E2 {but note Scot. reestet 'smoke-dried'}

reet - 'right' S2,T2,N2; pron. <u>rait</u> E3; **aareet?** standard
    greeting E3
rencky - 'great and boisterous' D1 Kennet as Yorx;
    renty 'fine' (of cattle, horses) NE1, 'well-
    shaped' (horses/cattle) NE2
rensh - 'to rinse' E2 [cf. Ice. <u>hreinsa</u>] cf. **range/sind**
rice - 'hedging wood' D1,NE2; 'brushwood' W2 [ON
    <u>hrīs</u>, OE <u>hris</u>]
riddy - 'ready' T2,S2,S3
RIDE: pret. **rade** W1,S2, **r'yad** S2
rife - 'ready, quick to learn' D1,NE2 [ON <u>rifr</u>]
rift - 'to belch; to plow up grassland' D1,NE2 [ON
    <u>ripta</u> 'to break up']
rig - 'to dress (oneself up)' S2
rigs - 'furrows in a field' T2; 'ridges' S2; **riggy**
    'ploughed into ridges' E2; "go the rig" - 'go
    straight ahead' T2 [OE <u>hrycg</u>, ON <u>hryggr</u>]
rind - 'frozen dew, hoar-frost' S2,D1 (+**rine**), E2
    [?OE <u>hrinde</u> ?'rime-frosted']
ripe - 'to rifle the pockets' T2; 'to steal privately'
    NE2; 'to quarry stones' S2; **rip** 'to rob or
    spoil' D1 [OE <u>rīpan</u>, 'to despoil']
RISE: pret. **riz** 'arose' N2
rive - 'to tear' D1,T2,NE2,S2,E2,E3,S3,N3; pret.**rave**
    S2; p.p.**rov(v)en** S2,E3 [MidE <u>ryve</u>, ON <u>rifa</u>]
road - 'way' e.g. "out of the road" E2 [OE <u>rād</u>]; **raad-
    hawder** 'car' E3; cf. **gate**
rolley - 'trolley, tram, four-wheeled vehicle'
    T2,NE2,E2,N2; 'tub' T3,E3; 'lorry' T3; [?<<u>roll</u>]
rook - '(thick) fog' + adj. **rooky** NE2,E2; **roaky** 'misty'
    S2 [?var. of <u>reek</u> < ON <u>reykr</u>]
roop - 'hoarseness' NE1; "a hoarsness and hoars
    voices occasion'd by a cold" D1 Kennet, NE2;
    roup 'a hoarseness' T2; **roopy** 'hoarse, husky'
    S2,E2 [*OED* s.v. <u>roup</u>]
roven - see **rive**
rowt - 'to bellow, roar' D1,NE1,NE2,T3; **rowting**
    'bellowing of an ox' NE2 [ON <u>rauta</u>]

rozzle - 'to beat, to redden' NE2; "he rozzled his hide" (by the fire) E2 [?<u><rose</u>]

ruddock - 'robin' S3 [OE <u>rudduc</u>]

RUN: pret. **they run** E3

runch - 'wild mustard/radish' D1,NE2; **runches** 'dry carlick' NE1; 'charlock when it is dry and withered' D1 Kennet as Northern

ryple - 'to lie, romance' D1 Kennet

s' - see SHALL

sackless - 'innocent, faultless' NE1; 'foolish, stupid' NE2,E2,E3; 'simple' T2; [ON <u>saklauss</u> 'innocent']

sall - see SHALL

SALT: **saut** S2,T2; **sawt (watter)** 'the sea' T1

sandlark - 'meadow pippit' E2

sands than <u>the beach</u> T3

sandscrawler - 'sand-martin' NE2

sanging-eather - see DRAGONFLY

Santy - 'Santa' T3,E3

sare/sair - 'sore' T2,S2,N2,T3,N3 **(saor)**; adv. 'greatly, very much' D1,S2,N2,T2, 'badly' W1 [OE <u>sār</u>]

sark - 'a shirt' D1 Kennet as Yorx, NE1,T1,T2,S2,E2; **top-sark** 'rough woollen over-shirt' (C'land) [OE <u>serc</u>, ON <u>serkr</u>]

satisfised - 'satisfied' E2

sauve - 'the sallow (Latin *salix*)' [i.e.'willow'] S2 [cf. Scot. <u>saugh</u>]

sc- - see also under **sk-**

scallions - 'young onions' E2,E3 [OFr <u>eschalogne</u> 'shallot']

scobbie - see CHAFFINCH

scon 'to strike' T2, 'to inflict punishment' NE2 cf.**scunner**

sconce - 'seat or bench' NE2,S3 [?Fr/Du]

sconce - 'a trick, pretence' N2 [slang]

scraffle - 'to slog away at' (a task) NE2,S2; 'to struggle for' T2, 'to compete for' NE2; 'to scramble' (C'land)

scrat - 'to scratch' (W3)

scribbly - see YELLOW-HAMMER

scribe - 'a jotting, a scribble' E2

scrike - see SHRIEK

scringe - 'to cringe' i.e. put teeth on edge E2

scrubbin' - 'rubbing (together)' N2

scrudged - 'squeezed' T2

scruff/scurf than dandruff

scrush - 'to crush' N3,E3,T3 [see *OED* s.v. craunch re initial s-]

scud (away) - 'to make haste' D1 Kennet as Yorx; "skudded 'em (balls in a game) aal ower" E3 [cf. Dan. skyde]

scudder - 'a beating' E3; vb. "skudded 'em" - 'beat them up' E3 {Wright s.v. skudge 'to buffet' as Scots} [cf. Du. schudden 'to shake']

scufter - 'to do fussily' S2

scumfish - 'to smother, to suffocate with smoke' NE2; 'to suffocate' (trans. e.g **scumfish'd**) S2,N3,E2,T2,S2,S3 [< discomfish]

scunner - 'to flinch, show signs of pain' E2; 'to notice, observe' T2; 'to shun' NE2 [cf.Scot. scunner, 'to feel disgust'; but Brockett as var. of shun] cf. **scon**

sea-coal - 'recycled coal from sea-shore' E3; 'coal from under the sea' E3 [cf. OE sǣ-col 'jet']

sea-fret - 'a wet mist or haze proceeding from the sea inland' NE2,E3; **fret** 'sea-mist' E3

seaves - 'rushes' D1,NE1,NE2 [ON sef]

seck - see SUCH

SEE: pret. **see'd** T2,S2,NE2

seea - see SO

seem'ly - 'seemingly', common for apparently E3

SELL: pret. **sell'd** S2,T2,E2; p.p. **selt** T2,E3,T3 [OE sellan 'to offer' is a weak verb, pret. selde]

119

sen - see SINCE

set - 'to put' E2; p.p. **setten** NE2; 'to propel a keel'
NE2; 'to accompany someone part of the
way' S2,N2; "set the table", than <u>lay</u> --; **set** 'a
punt-pole' D2

SEVEN: **sivin** E3; **seeven** T2

SEW: pret. **sowed** (corn) S2; but **sewed** (a seam) S2

shackle-b'yan - 'wristbone' S2,NE2 Brockett [from
fetters being applied to wrists]

shaling - 'scraping feet as you walk' S2

SHALL: **Ah s'** 'I shall' S2; **sall** S2 (+neg.
sannot),NE2,S2; pl. **we'se, ye'se** S2; pret.
suld 'should'; **sud** S2,T2,S2,N2,T2 (+**shud**)
[MidEN <u>sal</u>/<u>suld</u>, OE <u>sceal</u>/<u>sceolde</u>]

SHAPE: pret. **shap** S2 (+ noun)

sharen - 'cow-dung' NE2; **share** E2 [OE <u>scearn</u>]

SHE: **sheea** S2

shear - 'to reap or cut' NE2; **sheer** D1 [OE <u>scieran</u>]

sheelie - see CHAFFINCH

shibbin - 'leather shoe-lace' S2; cf. **wha(i)ng**

shiel - 'shelter' (whence <u>South Shields</u> etc.); 'a
circular hut of timber of turf; summer huts'
(Watson pp.49-50); 'temporary agricultural
living quarters' [?< ON <u>skjól</u> cf. OE <u>sciell</u>
'shell']

shift - 'shirt' T3

shire - 'to separate or pour off' NE2; 'to pour liquid
off a sediment' E2 [OE <u>scīran</u> 'to clarify']

shive - 'a slice' (of bread, etc) D1,NE2,S2,E2 [ON
<u>skifa</u>]

shool - 'a shovel' T2,S2 [cf. Du. <u>school</u>]

shoon - 'shoes' T2; **shun** S2,NE2,S2 [OE <u>scōn</u>, pl.]

shouther - 'shoulder' T2,S2,NE2; **shoother** T2,N2
[OE <u>schuldor</u>]

SHRIEK: **scrike** (vb/noun) S2,NE2,E2; **shrike** S3
[ON <u>skrik</u> 'a scream']

shuggy - 'a swing/to swing' e.g. "Give me a shuggy",
"He's shuggied all the afternoon" E2; **shuggy-**

shew 'a swing' (Robson, at a fair; Brockett, as improvised); **shuggy-boat** 'fairground swing' T3 [MidE shogge]

sic - see SUCH

siddle - 'to pick out the best' E2

sike - see **syke**

siller - 'silver' T2

sills - 'strata, of minerals' D1,NE2 [<OE/ON] cf. **syles**

SINCE: **sine** D1 Kennet as Yorx; **sin'** T2,S2,E2 Palgrave, where notes earlier **zyne**; **sen** S2,NE2,S2; **sin-syne** T2; "lang syne" W2 [MidENorth sen/sin]

sind - 'to rinse' (clothes) S2; 'to wash out/down' NE2 [MidE sind] cf. rensh

sipe - 'to seep, soak, drain' D1,NE2; 'to ooze out' S2; 'to leak' E2; 'to drain or extract' T2; **sipings** 'dregs' D1 [OE sypian] cf. **syke**

sk- - see also under **sc-**

skeel - 'milking-pail' D1,NE2; 'water-bucket' E2 [ON skjóla]

skeets - 'wooden runners for mine-shaft cage' N2; **skeets** 'boots' T3; **skeyt** 'a kite, scate' T2; **skyat** 'a paper kite' NE2 [?=skates, ON skata]

skelp - 'to slap with the open hand' D1,S2,NE2,T2; 'to strike smartly' T2,N2; 'to slap' E3 (+sexual connotation); 'a smacking blow' E2; **skelper** 'anything very large' NE2,E2 [cf. Ice. sklefa]

skemmy - 'common blue pigeon' E2,S3

skep - 'straw-basket' e.g. beehive S2,NE2,E3 [ON skeppa] cf. **skip**

skilly - 'oatmeal and water' T2 [?< skilligalee - C19th ship term]

skip - 'large tub esp. for winding coal up' [?ON skeppa, cf. Du. schipp, OE scip] cf. **skep**; **skipper** 'captain of a keel or coal-barge' T2,NE2 [cf. Du. schipper]

skirl - 'loud continuous scream or noise' D1,NE2

skinch - 'pax' (in children's play) E2,E3

skit - 'shit' E3 e.g. "took some skit"

skite - 'a quick exit' N2 [cf. Swed. skutta; ON skjóta 'to shoot (off)']

skitling - 'mischievous' E2 [<skittish]

skoit - 'to squirt'; 'to pee' E3

skooter - 'a squirter, syringe' T2

skr- see **scr-**

skugg - 'to hide' D1,NE2 [ON skugge 'shadow, shelter']

sky-yelpers - demon dogs riding through night sky D2

sladder - 'to spill' S3; **sladdery** 'muddy' S2,NE2,S3

slant - 'to mock or lie or dissemble' D1,NE2

slape - see SLIPPERY

slavvennin' - 'drooling' E3

slem - 'to work shoddily' S3

SLIDE: pret. **sl'yad** S2

SLIPPERY: **slape** NE1,S2,NE2 [ON slæipr]; **slippy** S2,NE2,E2

slocken - 'to put out or extinguish' D1; 'to slake, quench' NE2,S2,E2 [MidEN slockyn, ON slökva]

sloggers - 'trousers' T2; **to slogger** 'to walk with the stockings hanging loosely' E2; **sloggerin'** 'slovenly' S3 'untidy' NE2

slush - 'mire' S2; 'anything wet' NE2 [cf.Norw. slusk]; 'hard-working (person)' N2,N3; 'a heavy drinker' T2; 'heavy eater' NE2

SLY: **slee** S2,T2 [?ON slægr]

SMALL: **smaaly** S2 Dinsdale (+**smallish**), D1 Brockett ('little, puny'), N2,E2

smash - 'to crush' D1; "Od smash" (an oath) T1; **smash** 'a kind of oath among the pitmen' NE2 [cf. Norw. smaska 'to crush']

smatched - 'a bit burned, off-taste' S3,NE2 [OE smæċċan 'to taste of, smack of'; or smīcan 'to smoke']

122

smit - 'to infect' S2,NE2; 'an infection' NE2,E2,T3,E3
(esp."to get the smit"); **smittle** 'to infect' NE1,
'infectious' NE2,E2,S2 (as noun),'venemous'
D2 Brockie [OE smitte, 'pollution']
smush - (adj.) 'neat, smart' N2
smush - (vb.) 'to smoulder away' E2
snammy / snarter - see TURNIP
snaw - 'snow' D1,NE2,T2,S2,E3,etc. [MidEN snawe,
OE snāw]
snawk - 'to smell' D1 Kennet as Northern; **snoak** 'to
hide or nestle' T2; "snowkin' like pigs at a
sew" (C'land) [ON snoka 'to sniff at'] cf.
snook
snead - 'a handle' e.g. of a scythe D1 [OE snǣd]
sneck - 'a door-latch' NE2,E2,W2,E3; "sneck in
snout" - 'a spanner in the works' S3; **to sneck**
'to shut or latch a door' NE1,D1; 'to latch the
door' E2; 'to catch' E3 (cf.NE2 Brockett
"snedded a fish") [MidE sneck, 'latch', cf. OE
twī-snæċċe, 'two-pronged']
sned - 'to lop, cut' NE2; **sneddin'** 'fine line, small off-
cuts of fishing-line' E3 [OE snǣdan]
snedder - 'slim, slender' D1; **snether/snedder**
'slender' e.g. "a snether woman" D1
snell - 'sharp, cold' e.g. "a snell wind, a sharp
piercing wind" D1; 'sharp, keen' (e.g. air)
D1,NE2 [ON snjallr]
snig - 'an eel'; **sniggle** 'to fish for eels' NE2; **snigglies**
'wire noose for catching rabbits' E3 [see
OED, where snig = eel]
snite - 'to wipe' e.g. "snite your nose" D1 Kennet as
Yorx [ON snýta]
snod/snog - "smoothe, sleek as *He is snodly gear'd*"
D1 Kennet, NE2; **snod** 'a careful, close
person' T2; 'cunning' T2; 'to smooth down'
S2 (+p.p. **snodden**) [OE snīden 'with
haircut', cf. ON snoðinn 'bald']
snook - 'a headland' T3 [? = nose] cf. snawk

snotter - 'to snivel or cry' NE2; **snotter-clout** 'hanky' T2

snurls - 'nostrils' D1 Kennet as Northern

SO: **seea** S2,W3; **see** W2,N2; **sae** T1

sol-book - 'music book e.g. with the Psalms in' S2 [<u><sol-fa</u>]

someway - 'somewhere' T2

sonsy - 'nice, jolly-looking, stout' E2 Palgrave as from further North; 'lucky, pleasant, agreeable' T2,NE2 [?<Gaelic <u>sonas</u> 'good luck']

soo/sow - 'a tub with two ears to carry on a pole' D1 Kennet as Northern; **so(a)** NE1 [ON <u>sár</u>, OE <u>sā</u>]

soom - 'a swim' T2,W2; 'to swim' T2,NE2

soss - 'to lap up' (milk, of a dog etc) D1 Kennet as Yorx, NE2,S2; 'a mucky puddle' D1 Kennet as Northern; noun: 'a heavy clumsy fall' NE2; "he went down with such a soss" E2 [onom.]

spang-hew - 'to throw violently' S2,NE2; 'to fling e.g. a frog' (C'land); **spanghew'd** 'spread out, flattened' W2; **spangued out** 'forced out by pressure' N3, of a prop; **spangin'** 'jumping, [**spanghew**, cont.] leaping' T2 [*OED* s.v. <u>spanghew</u> 'to cause (a toad or frog) to fly into the air', < <u>spang</u> vb.2]

spaned - 'weaned' D1,NE2; **sp'yan** 'to wean' S2 [cf. Du. <u>spanen</u>, OFr <u>espanir</u>]

spanker - 'well-grown, big' S2 [cf. <u>spank</u> 'to go fast']

SPARROW: **dicky-hedgie** 'hedge-sparrow' E2; **hedger** E3; **spuggy** E2,E3,S3 [*OED* s.v. <u>sprug</u>]; **dirt-birds** 'any small (brown) bird' D2

SPEAK: pret. **spak** S2

speel - 'to climb' T2,NE2

speer - 'to enquire' E2 Palgrave as from further North; 'to seek, inquire' T2; **speir** 'to ask,

enquire, search out' NE1 [MidEN sper, OE
spyrian, 'to seek after' + ON spyrja]

spelk - 'the splints or splinters of wood used in
binding up of broken bones' D1; 'a splinter' +
'a small person' T2,N2, N3,E2,E3; 'a splint
for a broken limb' T3; **spell** 'a splinter'
NE1,NE2,S2,S3 (**+spelk**) [OE spelċ + ON
spela]

spennish - 'licorice' E2 [= spanish juice]

spew than vomit E2; cf. **puke**

spink - 'a spark of fire' D1,NE2; 'chaffinch' + 'a spark
of fire' S2 [cf. Low Gm. spink 'spot, freckle']
see also CHAFFINCH

sprag - 'an improvised brake' E2,N3

spreckled - 'speckled' S2,NE2 cf. **kenspecked**

sprent - 'bespattered' NE2, 'sprinkled' S2 [MidE
sprenge]

sprete - 'a pole, a long staff' D1 [OE sprēot]

sprog - 'to inform, sneak on s.one' E3

spuggy - see SPARROW

spurling - 'cartwheel rut' D1

squally-mashed - 'mangled' E3

squench - 'to quench' S2

staithe - 'a coal-drop for keels or ships' NE2 Brockett
(**+steeth**); **steeth** T2,E2 [ON stoð]

stanchil - 'iron window-bar' NE2 Brockett
(**+staneshel**); **stenchel** S2; **stainchils** 'door-
posts' NE2, **stenchels** E3; **door-staingels**
'door-frame' E2 [OFr estanchon]

stang / steng - 'a pole' NE2 Brockett [ON stöng]

stank - 'a pond' D2

stanie - 'stallion' E2 Palgrave (**styani**)

starrish - 'powerful, too strong' (of a drug, etc.) NE2
Brockett

stee - 'a ladder' NE1,D1,NE2,S2 [ON stige]

steek the heck - 'shut the door' D1,NE2; cf. **heck**

steer - '3-year old ox' D1,NE2; adj. 'strong (of voice)'
T1,E2

steeth - see **staithe**

steg - 'a gander' NE1,D1,S2,NE2; **steg & gyus** M/F T2
    [ON <u>steggi</u> 'a male bird']

stick - 'to (go on) strike' D2

stime - 'dim ray of light' S2; 'a faint glimpse' NE2
    [cf. Ice. <u>skíma</u>]

stirk - 'a yearling ox or heifer' D1,NE2; 'heifer, 1-2
    year old' S2; **sturk** 'a young bullock or heifer'
    D1; **quey-stirk** 'two-year-old heifer' E2 [OE
    <u>stirċ</u>, 'calf'] cf. **whey**

stite - 'sooner' e.g. "stite him as me" E2; **steit** "as well
    as" T2; **astite** "shortly, as soon" NE1 [<as
    tite] cf. **tit**

stithe/steith - 'stench, close atmosphere' E2; 'pungent
    smell' S2; **stythe** 'bad air' N3, **styth** 'foul air'
    T2; **stithe** 'hard, strong' D1 [?OE <u>stīð</u> 'sturdy'
    / ? Du. <u>stuive</u> 'dust']

stob - 'pointed stick' S2; 'post' T2,T3; 'post or stump'
    T2,NE2 [var. of <u>stub</u>]

stobbie/stubbie - 'unfledged bird' E2

stock - 'bed-frame' N2; **bed-stocks** S3

STOLEN (p.p.): **stown** S2, **stowen** T2

STONES: **stanes** T1, **styens** T2,N2, **staen** T2

storken - 'to congeal' D1,NE2,S2 [ON <u>storkna</u>]

stot - 'young bullock or steer' NE1; 'an ox 2-3 year
    old' D1,NE2,S2; [ON <u>stútr</u> cf. MidE <u>stot</u>];
    Stot-Plough 'Plough Monday' NE2 Brockie re
    Hartlepool

stot - 'to bounce' T3; 'to make bounce' T3,E3; trans.
    'to make bounce' / intrans. 'to rebound' NE2;
    'knock (someone) down' E3; **stotty balls** 'a
    ball game' S3; **stottie** 'round, flat loaf' E3;
    stottie-cake 'flat loaf' (oven-bottom bread) T3
    cf. **fadge** [?Dutch <u>stuiten</u>, 'to bounce,
    rebound']

stound - 'numbing pain of a blow' S2 [cf. OE
    <u>stunian</u>]

stour(e) - 'disturbance, commotion' W1; 'dust' D1,S2; 'dust/confusion' T2; 'dust in motion' NE2,E2, 'dust floating in the air' T2; **stoory** 'dusty' NE2 [MidEN **stour(es)**]

STRAIGHT: **strite** T2,N3, **stright** S2, **strike** N2

stramash - 'ruin, destruction' S2,NE2 (+vb 'to destroy') [onom.?]

stramp - 'to trample' NE2,E2 [OED as Scots but cf. Gm. strampfen]

stravagin' - 'wandering' T2; **stravaigin'** T2 [?<extravage]

STREAK/STRETCH: **streek** 'to stretch or lay out' NE2; **streak** 'to stretch (s.thing)' S2, pret. **struke** S2 [?OE strīcan, intrans.]

STRIKE: pret. **streaik** 'struck, tossed' W2

stumor - 'an unusual person, someone stupid' T3; 'a bad lot' T3; 'an incompetent or stupid person' E3 [OED connects with meaning 'sham']

SUCH: **sicken** W1; **seck** NE2,W2 e.g."seck a yan"; **sic** NE2,T2,T3; **sike** NE1,S2 (+sik-like); **suchen** e.g. "suchen a one" E2 [OE swilċ, ON slíkr]

sud/suld - see SHALL

sump - 'a puddle' S2, 'drainage for water at bottom of pit shaft' N3; 'an undercutting' (via Heslop)

sup - 'a drop (to drink)' E2; also vb. 'to drink' E2

swale - 'windy, cold, bleak' NE1; "cold or bleak air, as to lie in the swale" (sleep in the open) D1 Kennet [ON svalr 'cool'; Wright gives as 'shady place in open', E.Mids, EA] cf. **sweal**

swalley - 'a dip or hollow' N2 Barrass (in a mine-tunnel), E2,N3 [?ON svelgr / ?OE ġeswelg]

swameish - 'shy, bashful' D1,NE2 [?squeamish]

swang - 'green bottom' NE1; 'same as letch' D1; 'swamp' T2

swarth - 'the spirit or ghost of a dying man' D1 Kennet C'land, NE2; **sward** D1 [?swarthy]

sweal - 'to singe or burn, to waste or blaze away' D1
Ray (+**swale**); 'to gutter or flare' (of a candle),
"as proverbial saying in the north, see how
the candle sweals" D1 Kennet, **sweel**, E2,
sweal, T1; **sweal** 'to diminish' (e.g. of a
candle flame) S2; **sweal/sweadle** 'to waste
away as candle in wind' S3; **sweel** 'to melt,
waste away' T2; 'to burn away rapidly' NE2
[OE <u>swǣlan</u>, 'to burn']

swere - "dull, heavy, as, a swere fellow" D1;
'unwilling, burdensome' NE2 [OE <u>swǣr</u>]

swiney - 'common sow-thistle' E2

syles - 'principal rafters of a house' D1 [= sill]

syke - 'a small brook' D1,NE2; **sike** 'ditch, water-
channel' S2 [ON <u>sík</u>] cf. **sipe**

t' - 'the' S2,W2,W3 {cf.Lancs}; **'t** 'it' e.g. "he gave me't"
E2

tabs - 'cigarettes' E3,T3 [after <u>Ogden's Tabs</u>, a brand
name]

tadger - 'a child' E3

taggerman - 'scrapman' E3 [?< <u>tagger</u> 'tinned sheet
iron']

taistrel - 'a rude or prankish kid' E2,NE2 Brockett
(+**testril**) [?=a sixpence]

TAKE: **tak** D1,NE2,T1,S2, **tyek** T2,N2, **taek** T2; pret.
teuk N2, **tuke** S2, **teeak** S2; p.p. **took** E3,
ta'en 'taken' W1,T2; **t'yan** S2; **tyen** T2;
tyun/chun E3; **teun** N2,E2,E3, **teean** S2

tallyman - 'any due collector' E3 e.g. instalment
collector; **tallystick** 'notched record of dues'
W2

tappy-lappy - 'pell-mell' NE2,E2

tara/tata than <u>goodbye</u> E3

tarry towt - 'tarry cord' N3; 'single strand of rope
steeped in tar' E2; 'thick treated string used
to tie hewer's token to tub' E3

tatie - see POTATO

tave - 'to walk laboriously' e.g. over a ploughed field
S2 (**t'yav**); **teeave** 'to be awkward' S2; **taav** 'to
wade in mud' S3; **taving** 'delirious or
random motion' NE2 [cf. Norw. <u>tava</u> 'to toil']

taum - 'a fishing line made of hair' D1; **towm** W2;
tawm/tome/tam 'twine' etc. NE2 [ON <u>taumr</u>
'cord/line']

taws - 'fancy marbles' N2,E2; **taw** 'the shooting
marble' S2,E2

ted - see TO / **teea** - see TOE

teejy - 'tedious, peevish' E2

teem - 'to pour (down,out)' NE1,S2,E2; **team** 'to
empty, pour out' D1,NE2 [ON <u>tomme</u> cf. OE
<u>tōm</u> (adj.)] cf. **toom**

TELL: pret. **tell'd** 'told' T1,S2,NE2,N2; **tell'd/telt**
S2,T2,E2, **telt** T2 [MidEN <u>telled</u>]

temse - 'a sieve, to sieve' S2,NE2 (+**timse**) [OE
<u>temesian</u> (vb)]

teng - 'to sting' D1 Kennet as Yorx,S2: p.p. **tenged**;
tenging-ether 'large dragonfly' S2, **tanging-
nadder** NE2 [ON <u>tange</u> 'a point']

teum - see **toom** / **teun** - see TAKE / **teup** - see
tup

tew - 'to tire, mess about' D1,S2,E2,S3,E3 e.g. "tew
someone"; 'to tumble about, ruffle, rumple'
[**tew**, cont.]
T3 Dobson as archaic; 'to struggle, toil' T2;
tue 'to work hard', **tuing** 'tiring, fatiguing,
hard-working' NE2; 'energetic' T1; **tewing**
'tiring' N3 (+p.p. **tewed**); "couldn't be tewed
with.." - 'not bothered with..' E3; "sair tews" -
'hard work' T2 [OE <u>tāwian</u> 'to work on,
harrass']

tha - see THEY / **thou**

that (gen.rel.): 'that/which/who'; **ed** W2; **thit** N2
[MidEN <u>that</u>, OE <u>þæt</u>]

thaw, thee - see **thou**

THEIR: **thor** T1,N2; **ther** S2

THEM: **thame** 'they/them' T1; - see also THOSE

THERE: **thar** N2; **thor** N2

THESE: **thir** W1,S2; **thur** D1 Kennet as Yorx, NE2;
    thor T1,NE2; **thease** S2 [ON þeir]

THEY: **tha** N2; **them** E3 e.g. "them was walkin'
    around"

thir - see THESE

thon - 'yonder' T2; **thon's** 'that is' T3;
    thonder/yonder T2 {thon, D'm, yon,
    Cleveland, Yorks} [thon formed by analogy
    with yon?]

thor - see THEIR/THERE

THOSE: **them** N2,E3,etc.

thou: 'you' (sg.) T1,S2,N3; **thoo** N2,T2,W2,E2,T3 as
    familiar, **tha** S2 [OE þū] {thoo is the
    expected D'm form, ye for sg. is typical of
    T/N'land, but also you sg. after standard
    English}; **tha** 'thee' (acc.sg.) S2,N3, **te** T2,
    thou/the' T1 [OE þē]; **thee** 'thine' W2,N2,
    thei N2; **thaw** T2,N2; **thahne** 'yours' S2 [OE
    þīn]; **theesell** 'yourself' T2,N3

thrang - 'a throng' T2,S2; adj. 'overcrowded'
    S2,NE2,S2,E3, **throng** E2, **thrung** T3 [<vb.
    thring < OE þringan]

thraw - 'to twist, writhe' NE2; **thrawn** 'thrown' T2
    [OE þrāwan]

threap - 'to blame, rebuke' NE1; **threep** 'to assert
    positively' T2; "threeps doon it is" - 'insists it
    is' T2; 'to protest, argue' T2 [OE þrēapian 'to
    rebuke']

thropple - 'windpipe' NE1,T2,S2,NE2,E2

throstle - 'thrush' E2,S3; [OE þrostl]

thrum - 'a hank of wool' E3; verb 'to purr' T3 Dobson
    [both meanings in Wright; cf. threethrums
    'purrs' T2, onom.]

thunner-pash - 'thunder-shower' S2,W2; **thunner-
    stane** 'quartz pebble' S2

tid - see TO

tied - 'bound' (to do s.thing) S2,E2

tiggy - 'game of touch' E2; **tig** NE2

til - 'to' S2, of place,W1 (+**until**) {NE2 Brockett gives to/unto as esp. N'land} [MidEN til her = to her, etc. < ON til]

tin, tiv - see TO

tipcat - 'knurr & spell, knocking a small stick in the air with a longer stick and then trying to hit it' S3

tite - 'soon, easily, well' NE2; **as tite** 'as soon' i.e. 'rather' D1; **titter** 'sooner, rather' D1,NE2 [ON títt] cf. **stite**

TO/TOO: **te** T2,N2,S2,W2,N3,etc (+ sense of 'as/for' e.g. "a sossenger te the' supper" W2; **tee** T2, **ti** S2; **tin** (before vowel) S2,E2; **tiv** (before vowel) T2,NE2,N2,T3; **tev** W2; **tid** 'to it' N2, **tud** W2, **tit** S2; **ted** 'to the' W2, **tud** W2; **turus** 'to us' E3 [OE tō, 'to/for/as'] cf. **til**

TOAD: **taed** T2; **t'yad** S2; **tyed** T2 [OE tāde]; **paddock** D1 Kennet (as 'a young frog'), NE2 Brockett (+**paddick**), T2 [ON padda 'toad']

TOBACCO: **backy** T2,N2; **bako** T2

tod - see FOX

TOE: **teea** S2; **teah** S2 [OE tā]

toitle - see **towp**

toom - 'empty' D1 Ray (+**tume**),T3 (+**tyum**); **tum** 'empty' D1, **tume** T2; **teum** N2,E2 (+'workless'); **tyum/chum** E3; **tiummun** 'empty one' (i.e. tub) N3 [ON tómr cf. OE tōm] cf. **teem**

toom - 'to card' (wool) D1

toop - see **tup**

TOOTHACHE: **tyoothwark** E2; **tuithwark** T2 [ONorthumb.warc 'pain'] cf. **hedewark** s.v. HEAD

toppin' - 'crest e.g. of bird, or human hair' S2 cf. place-name, Roseberry Topping

131

torfle - 'to fall down and die' NE2; 'to founder, to
  fall, to die' (of animals) NE2 Brockett
  (**+torfel**) #source
tother - see OTHER
towm - see **tawm**
towp/toitle - 'to upset' S3
toyte 'to totter as though old' T2
TREAT: pret./p.p. **tret** 'treated' N2,T3,E3
trig - 'neat, trim' NE2; "trigged out" - 'dressed
  smartly' S2 [ON tryggr 'dependable']
trod - 'a footpath' D1,NE2,S3
troon - 'a mason's trowel' E2
trow - 'trough' S2,E2
tud - see TO / **tufit** - see LAPWING
tug - 'to rob' (a bird's nest) E2
tum - see **toom** 'empty'
tup - 'ram' D1 Kennet as Yorx (**+teup**); **teup** 'tup,
  ram, decorative tub' N2; 'ram' E2; **tupe** 'a
  ram' S2, **teeap** S2; **tyup/yow** M/F T2; **tyup**
  'the last basket or corf sent up out of the pit
  at the end of the year, accompanied by a
  tup's horn, which usually marks each score'
  T2 [MidE tupe] cf. **buss**
TURNIP: **bagie** T3; **snammy** T3; **snarter** E3 [cf. ON
  snart 'sharp,strong']; **turmit** T2,NE2, **tormit**
  T2,NE2
twang - 'dialect, pronunciation' E3; "for everlasting
  twang" - 'for ever and ever' T2;
twank - 'to bang' T3; 'to spank' E3 [onom.]
twat - 'female genitalia' E3
twee - see TWO
twing - 'fretful, uneasy' S2 [cf. ModE twinge]
twinny - 'either of a pair or twins' E3; "twee
  twinnies" - 'both twins' T2;
twist - 'to complain, whinge' esp. **twisting**
  'discontented' E2 (+adj.**atwist**), E3 (**+twisty**)

132

twitch-bell - 'earwig' S2,NE2,E2; **twitchy-bell** E3
[?<u>twich</u> 'tongs' cf. presumed OE *twīcele,
'forked', or from <u>twitch</u> 'wheat']

TWO: **twa** W1; **twee** T2,W2; **tweah** S2, **tweea** D1,S2;
"atween the twee leets" - 'at twilight' T2
{pron. <u>too</u>, most D'm; <u>twee</u> W, <u>tweea</u>
S/Cleveland, <u>twa</u>/<u>tway</u> Scot.} [MidEN <u>twa</u>
OE <u>twā</u>];

twocker - 'car-thief, joy-rider' e.g. "D/side twocker
squad" (E3 graffiti)

tyke - 'a dog' D1 Kennet as Yorx,T2; 'a blunt or
vulgar fellow' NE2 [ON <u>tík</u> 'female dog']

tyum - see **toom**

un- check simplex (unprefixed) form

unlarn'd - see **learn**

unpatient - 'impatient' NE2,E2

up-aheight - 'up in the air' E3; **up-aheyte** T3; **up-
aheet** W2,W3

up-cast - 'to throw up/back' E2,E3; "cast up at s.one"
- 'reproach' S3; **upkest** 'to reproach' NE2
[MidEN <u>kest...up</u>] cf. **kessen**

up-grown - 'adult' E2

up home - 'back home' E3

urchin - 'hedghog' S2 {thus S; N: <u>hedghog</u>} [OFr
<u>hericon</u>]

urled - 'pinched with cold' S2

US: **uz/huz** 'me' T2; 'us' T2,N2; **huz** S2,NE2

vally - 'value' E2

a vast - 'a large number' (of s.thing) E2

VERY: **varra** 'very' W2; **varry** T2,S2,T3; **vera** T2;
varra/varry/vurry NE2; **varney** 'very near'
N3,E3,T3

vine - 'a pencil' E2,E3,T3; **keely-vine** 'a black-lead
pencil' NE2 [?from use of vine charcoal to
write with? cf. *OED* s.v. <u>vine-black</u>]

wad - see WILL

waff - 'a slight puff of wind' NE2; 'rush of air' T3; 'waft' E3; "a waff o'cawd" - 'a slight draught' T2; **waft** 'the spirit or ghost of a dying man' D1 Kennet as Yorx, D2 Brockie (+**waff**); **waff** S2,NE2 [cf. Norw. veift 'a puff of wind']

Wagga - 'Longhill area of Hartlepool' S3

wairsh - 'tasteless' T2,T3; **warsh** E2; **worsh** E3; **wairch** 'insipid' T2,NE2 (+**wairsh**); **walch** 'insipid' NE1, **walsh** S3; Wright as 'lacking salt' [*OED* s.v. wersh]

walsh - 'showery' (day) S2,S3 (+'insipid')

wang-tooth - 'canine tooth' NE1; 'molar' NE2 [OE wong-toð i.e. 'cheek-tooth']

wankle - 'wobbly, wavery' NE1 Ray; 'loose, limber, fickle, change-able' e.g. of weather D1; 'unstable' S2 'uncertain' D1,NE2; 'weak, tottering' W2 [OE wancol]

want - see MOLE

wappies - 'wasps' {Upper Tyne}

war - see BE / **wark** - see WORK

wark - 'to ache' NE1,S2,E2,T2,NE2; **werke** "to ake or pain, as my head werkes, my teeth werke" D1 [ONorthumb. in this sense]

WARRANT: **warnd** 'to warrant, be certain' N2; **warned** T2,NE2

warsel - see WRESTLE

watchee - 'a watchman' E3; cf. **gadjee**

Water-waggie - 'inhabitant of Cold Hesledon' E3 [re water works]

wath - 'a ford' S2,NE2 [ON vað]

waxin' - 'growing' T2 [OE wēaxan]

WAY: in conj. phrase "that way on..." - 'in that case...' E3

waysgoose - 'day trip from a firm' E2

wedger - 'anything large or outsize' N3

weel - 'well' W1,S2,T2,NE2,S2

weeny - 'tiny' S2,E2,E3; **weans** 'children, little ones'
    T2,NE2,E3 [<u>wee</u> <ONorthumb. w<u>æ</u>ġ 'a
    quantity']
weet - 'wet' NE2,T2 Robson ('or rain'),S2
werke - see **wark**
wesh - 'to wash' S2,T2,W2,N3 etc.
whang - 'a leather thong' D1, 'small leather thong,
    leather belt' NE2; **whaing** 'shoe-lace' E2;
    wh'yang S2; **whang** 'a sharp blow' T2; 'a
    large piece or share' S2 [var. of <u>thwang</u>
    'thong']
what for... - 'why...?' E2
what'n/what'na... - 'what kind of...?' E2
whe - see WHO
wheezles - 'the wheezes' N2; vb. 'to wheeze' S2,NE2
WHELK: **willik** E3; **wilk/whilk** 'periwinkle or sea-
    snail' NE1; **willok** 'periwinkle' T3; 'winkle'
    T3 [OE <u>weoloc</u>]
whemmle - 'to up-turn a container' S2,W2,NE2
    (+**whommel/whummel**) [<<u>whelm</u>]
whey stirk / quey - 'a two-year heifer' D1,E2 {Scot.
    <u>quey</u>}; **why** 'a heifer or young cow until it
    has had a calf' NE2; **steerk/why** as M/F T2
    [ON <u>kviga</u>]
WHICH: **whichen**, as in "whichen a one" E2; **whilk**
    'who, which, what' S2; 'somebody, a certain
    person' D1; 'which' T2,NE2 [OE <u>hwilċ</u>]
whiles - adv. 'at times' N2; 'sometimes' NE2,E2,W2;
    'occasionally' T2; conj. 'until' NE2,E3
    [MidEN]
whin - 'furze, gorse' S2,E2; **whins** NE2; **whinny-
    bushes** E3 (Crimdon) [cf. Swed. <u>hven</u>]
whinge - 'to whine, complain' S2,NE2; **wingeing**
    E2,E3
whisht - 'hush!' E2 Palgrave as N'land, NE2; **whisht**
    'hushed' S2; **eesht!** (sound of disapproval) E3

WHO: **whe** T1,T2,NE2 (+**whee**), N2,E3; **whee** W2;
wheah, weea S2; **whese** 'whose' T2, 'who
is...?' E3 [OE hwā]
why-aye - 'to be sure!' E2,E3,T2 Hull (+**by-ay**); **wia**
S2, **wya** NE2, **whyah** S2; **eigh-wye** NE2
wick - 'live i.e. of a raw cut' E2; **whick** - 'live e.g.
whick-hedge' S2,NE2 [MidEN whik, OE
cwić 'living']
wickens - 'creeping grass' NE2,E3; **quickens** D1
[from previous?]
wife - 'wife/woman' NE2,E2,E3 (+**wifie**) [OE wīf, of
any woman]
WILL: **will** prefered to shall E2; **Aw'll** T2, **A'l** S2;
winnet 'will not' T2, **weeant** S2; **winnot** S2,
winna/winnit N2,T3; **winna/winnot** NE2
{Palgrave says **winnot** used absolutely or
before vowel, **winna** before consonant}; pret.
wad 'would' S2,T2,E2,N2,S2,etc.; **wud** W2;
wid N2; **A'd** S2; neg. **wad-n't** S2, **waddent**
T2;
willik - see WHELK
win - 'to get' NE2,D1 e.g. stones in a quarry; pret.
wan S2 [OE ġewinnan]
WIND ('to twist' etc): pret. **wand** S2
wind-berry - 'a whortle-berry or Bill-berry' D1
Kennet as Northern
winge - see **whinge**
wirsle - 'to exhange, change' (coins etc) D1 Kennet as
N'land [OE wrixlan]
wist - see **wot**
wite - 'to reprehend, blame' D1 Kennet as
Northern,NE2; noun, 'blame' E2; **white** 'to
requite' NE1 (+'to blame'), NE2 [OE wītan]
WITH: **wi'/wiv** S2,T2,N2,T2; **wuth/wu** W2; **wid** 'with
it' T2; **win** before vowel S2,T2,E2 {Palgrave
says **win** before short vowel, **wiv** before long
vowel; Brockett gives **wiv** as D'm/N'land, **wi'**
as Yorx, **wud** as C'land}

136

wiz - see BE
wobbit - see BUT
WOE: **wae** T2; 'woeful' W1; **weah** 'sorry, unhappy'
    S2; **wea** NE2 [OE wā]
WOMB: **wame** - 'belly' T1,S2, **w'yam** NE2
wor - see OUR
worme - 'dragon' NE2,D2 [OE wyrm 'reptile,
    dragon']
wot - 'to know, guess' T2; 'to know' NE2; **wat** 'reckon'
    W1; **wist** 'knew' W1; **wist** (noun)
    'knowledge/news' W1 [OE witan/witt]
WORK: **wark** T2,S2,N2; **wark-folk** 'labourers'
    S2,NE2; cf. **waak** 'walk'
wowl - 'to howl/cry' T2,NE2,E2
wraut - 'a wart' S2
WRESTLE: **russle** N2; 'to move up and down, to goe
    backward and forward' D1 Kennet as
    Northern; **warsel** 'to struggle' T2; 'to strive,
    wrestle' NE2; **worsel** 'wrestle' T2
WRONG: **rang** N2 etc
wrowt out - 'worn out' T2 [<wrought]
wunn - 'to dwell' e.g. "where woon you?" NE1 Ray
    (+**wonne**), D1 Kennet; **woon/wun** NE2 [OE
    wunian]

yable - 'able' T2,W2; **yabble** S2; **yebble** N2,N3
yacker - 'acre' S2; see also **pit-yacker**
yade - 'a horse' D1 Kennet as Northern, NE2; **yad** 'a
    worn-out horse' T2; **yaud** 'a horse' D1 Kennet
    as Yorx, NE1,S2, **yaude** D1 [ON jalda 'a
    mare']
yaits - 'oats' D1
yak - see OAK
yal - 'ale' D1,S2,NE2,S2,E3,T3; **yell** T2,N2,T3
yam - see HOME
yammer - 'to cry like a dog in pain' D1; 'to complain,
    fret' NE2,T2; 'whine' T3; "yammer on" - 'to

scold' etc T2,E3 [cf. OE ġēomrian, MidDu.
jammer]

yan - see ONE / **yance** - see ONCE

yare - 'sharp, ready' of people D1, NE1 (+'nimble'),
NE2 [OE ġearwe]

yare - 'a weir', "absolutely abounds in Co.Durham
records" (Jackson *Place-Names of Durham*,
1916 p.71.)

yark - 'to lash, beat' S2,T3; 'to wrench, twist, jerk
s.thing' NE2; 'to beat, to go quickly' T2; 'a
sharp blow' T3; **yerk** 'to thresh' i.e. 'thrash'
T2 [MidE yerk]

yat - see GATE

ye - 'you' (pl.) T1,S2,N2,W2,E3 (Tyneside uses **ye** for
sg. thou, so too N2,N3,E3; after Irish/L'pool
there is a tendency to create a new pl., **ye's**)
[OE ġē]

year than years, as pl. e.g. "six year" E3; **eers** N2 [OE
neut.pl. gear(u), but many measurements
used in sg. e.g."20 mile"]

yearth - see EARTH

yebble - see ABLE

yecky - 'an echo' T2

yell - see **yal**

YELLOW: **yallow** S2; see also **blake**

YELLOW-HAMMER: **yowley** E2; **yellow-yowley** T2;
scribbly E3 [re its eggs]

yep - 'ape' T2; cf. **aup**

yetling - 'a small pot' E2 [MidE yet 'to pour', cf. OE
ġēotan]

yeuk, yewk - see **yuke**

yewer - see HEWER

yewd, yod - see GO

yit - 'yet' T2

yon - 'that' (demonst.) W1,E2; adv. **yonder** NE1,E2,
yonner T2; **yont** 'beyond' T2 [OE ġeon]

young 'un than youngster E3

yowk - see howk

138

yowl - 'to howl' D1 Kennet as
Northern,T2,S2,NE2,E3; **youl** 'to howl like a
dog' D1 [Wright as 'to yelp'; but originally
variant of howl?]

yowley - see YELLOW-HAMMER

yowster - 'to fester' D1 Kennet as Northern; **yowfter**
NE1 Ray (as misprint) [OE ġeolster 'a sore']

yoxing - 'the hickup' D1 Kennet as Yorx [OE
ġeocsian]

yuke - 'to itch' D1; **yuck** NE1; **yeuk** (n/vb) S2,NE2;
yewk/yuck 'to itch, to have an itching in the
skin' D1; **yucking** T1 [MidE yeke, cf. MidDu.
jeuken]

Yule - 'Xmas' T2,NE2,E2; **yule-doo** 'yule-dough or
doll: gingerbread man with hands joined in
front' E2,E3,T3; **huildoo** 'pastry made for
children at Christmas' T2; **heul doo** N2;
yoodle-doo 'Xmas box to putter' E3; **yule-
clog** 'Yule-log' S2,NE2,S2,E2,W2 [OE Ġēol]

yuly - 'tender' T2; **yulley** 'whimpering' S3; cf. **huly**
'peevish, fretful' D1 Kennet [ON hógligr?]

yuvven - see OVEN

General Bibliography

ALLAN, Thomas (ed.) *Allan's Tyneside Songs* (1862)

ANDERSON, J.J. (ed.) *Records of Early English Drama: Vol.7 Newcastle on Tyne* (Toronto, 1982) Transcripts of Livery Companies' records of miracle play performances C16-17th.

ANGUS: *Angus's Newcastle Garland* (1805)

ARMSTRONG, Thomas (The Pitman's Poet) *Song Book compiled by his own son W.H.('Poetry')* Armstrong (2nd edn, Chester-le-Street, 1930)

ARMSTRONG: *Polisses & Candymen: The complete works of Tommy Armstrong, the pitman poet* ed. Ross Forbes (Consett, 1987)

BAILEY, John *General View of the Agriculture of the County of Durham* (1810) Includes 'A glossary of provincial terms', also reprinted as a pamphlet.

BARMBY, J. (ed.) *Memorials of St Gile's, Durham* (Surtees Soc. vol.95, 1895) Includes (pp.9-122) accounts of the Grassmen's Company from 1579 to 1782 - mostly standard English but some few dialect forms.

BARRASS, Alexander *The Pitman's Social Night* (Consett, 1897, repr. Seaham 1993 ed.Bill Griffiths) Dialect songs on the work and life of a mining community.

BEE, Jacob *Diary* pp.45-66 in Surtees Society vol.118 (1910) A diary covering 1681-1717, with occasional local forms.

BELL, John (ed.) *Rhymes of Northern Bards* (1st edn, 1812; repub. with intro. by David HARKER, Newcastle 1971)

BELL: *Songs from the Manuscript Collection of John Bell* ed. D.I.HARKER, Surtees Society vol.196 (1985)

BLAKEBOROUGH, Richard *Wit, Character, Folklore & Customs of the North Riding of Yorkshire* (London, 1898)
Includes dialect prose and verse, and extensive glossary.

BLAKEBOROUGH, Richard *T'Hunt o' Yatta Brigg* (Guisborough, 1896)

BLENKINSOPP, R.W. *The Teesdale Dialect* (Barnard Castle, 1931)
Lists Old Norse-derived words (without etymologies though), and a brief phonology; then extensive glossary, though somewhat dependent on previous work.

BROCKETT, John T. *A Glossary of North Country Words, with their Etymology, and Affinity to other Languages; and occasional notices of local customs and popular superstitions* (2 vols, Newcastle, 1846)
Comprehensive word-list, but with many of its examples drawn from literary sources and previous glossaries; new material for Newcastle only.

BROCKIE, Wm *Legends and Superstitions of Co.Durham* (Sunderland, 1886)

CHICKEN, Edward *The Collier's Wedding. A poem* (1764. etc., repr. Seaham 1995 ed.Bill Griffiths)
Poem about the impact of the new mining class on Newcastle.

CROCKER, Jean (compiler) *Accent on the North-East: Dialect jottings* (Darlington ca.1983)
Local material, words, phrases, games etc.

CUTHBERT: *The Life of St Cuthbert in English Verse ca. AD 1450 from the Original Manuscript in the Library at Castle Howard* Surtees Society vol.87 (1891)

DINSDALE, Frederick T. *A Glossary of Provincial Words used in Teesdale in the Co. of Durham* (London, 1849)
Covers Middleton in Teesdale to Darlington, and north of Tees for 9 or 10 miles.

DOBSON, Scott *The Geordie Dictionary* (Newcastle 1974)

EDWARDS, V.K. et al. *The Grammar of English Dialects: A survey of research* (pamphlet, London 1984)
Excellent survey of recent work, with extensive bibliography. Important for its warning against rejecting 'slang', which is potentially dialect in creation, and for its consideration of the problems dialect speakers face in learning English at school.

EGGLESTONE, Wm Morley *Betty Podkin's Visit to Auckland Flower Show: An amusing narrative in the Weardale Dialect* (Stanhope, 1876)
"..when yan gans away inted world yan gits yan's een op'n'd"

EGGLESTONE, Wm Morley *Betty Podkin's Letter ted Queen on Cleopatra's Needle written ed Wardle dylect by Peter Podkins, Jun.* (London, 1877)

EGGLESTONE, Wm Morley *Weardale Names of Field and Fell* (Stanhope, 1886)
Survey of geographical feature names.

ELLIS, Stanley 'Scandinavian Influences on Cumbrian Dialect', pp.161-7 in *The Scandinavians in Cumbria* ed. John R. Baldwin & Ian D. Whyte (Edinburgh, 1985)

Looks at possible Viking-derived word-survival in central Cumbria and Pennines.

EMBLETON, D. *Local Dialect Dialogues* (ca.1897)
Short Geordie pieces, often medical/morbid, good annotations.

FALLAW, H.F. *The Tyneside Tongue* (Gateshead, 1915)
Poetic fantasia on dialect details.

FLOM, George T. *Scandinavian Influence on Southern Lowland Scotch: A contribution to the study of the linguistic relations of English and Scandinavian* (Columbia Univ. Germanic Studies vol.1 no.1, New York 1900)
Assessment of Viking influence on pronunciation and vocabulary; also relevant to Noth-East.

GIBSON, Alexander C. *The Folk-Speech of Cumberland* (London 1880)
Poems and stories in various Cumberland sub-dialects; glossary.

GIL, Alexander *Logonomia Anglica, quæ Gentis sermo faciliùs addiscitur* (1619, 2nd edn 1621)
Early work on spelling, etymology, grammar, with list of Northern words.

GREEN, John *Tales & Ballads of Wearside* (4th edn, London 1885)
Stories, mostly in standard English, but with a few dialect (Sunderland) items.

HESLOP, R. Oliver *Northumberland Words* (English Dialect Society vol.31, London, 2 vols, 1892-4)
Extensive coverage, including mining terms etc., but little detail.

HESLOP, R. Oliver *A Bibliographical List of Works Illustrative of the Dialect of Northumberland* (English Dialect Society, vol.43, 1896)

HULL, J.E. "A Grammar of Tyneside" *Vasculum* 8
(1922) 55-60, 105-7, 117-21
Article covering most aspects of Geordie grammar,
relating to period 1870-90.

KASTOVSKY, Dieter "Scandinvian influence"
pp.320-336 in *The Cambridge History of the English
Language* vol.1 ed. R.M.Hogg (1992)

KERSWILL, Paul E. *Social and Linguistic Aspects of
Durham (e:)* (pamphlet, ?1983)

KOLB, Edward *Phonological Atlas of the Northern
Region* (Bern 1966)

LAWSON, Jack *A Man's Life* (London, 1932, 1944)
Autobiography with some references to dialect
development in Co.Durham in the late C19th.

LEE, John *Weardale Memories and Traditions*
(Consett, 1950)

McINTOSH, Angus et al. (eds.) *A Linguistic Atlas of
Late Medieval England* (4 vols, Aberdeen, 1986)
Word-maps. Includes list of documents for the
County at vol.III pp.92-7

MARSHALL, John (ed.) *The Northern Minstrel*
(1806)
Collection of dialect songs, with a radical and
popular tone.

MARSHALL, John (ed.) *A Collection of Songs,
Comic, Satirical, and Descriptive, Chiefly in the
Newcastle Dialect, and illustrative of the language
and manners of the common people on the banks of
the Tyne and neighbourhood* (Newcastle, 1827)

MAWER, Allen *The Place-Names of
Northumberland & Durham* (Cambridge, 1920)

MERITON, George *A Yorkshire Dialogue* (1683, repr. Yorks.Dialect Soc. as Reprint 2, 1959, ed A C Cawley)

MOORMAN, F.W. (ed.) *Yorkshire Dialect Poems 1673-1915* (London 1916)
Interesting anthology, with thorough introduction

MUSGROVE, Frank *The North of England: A history from Roman times to the present* (Oxford, 1990)

OLIVER, William (ed.) *A Collection of Local Songs, Poems etc.* (Newcastle, 1829)
Works of a light, humorous type.

ORTON, Harold *The Phonology of a South Durham Dialect: Descriptive, historical, and comparative* (London, 1933)
Study of dialect of Byers Green (nr. Bishop Auckland), a mining village, but whose traditional dialect "has advanced very far along the path of disintegration" (p.xvii) due to elementary education, growth of intercommunication and immigration from other areas. Detailed study of sounds, plus a few verbatim conversations (p.185ff).

ORTON, Harold et al. (eds.) *The Linguistic Atlas of England* (London 1978)
Word maps, based on survey of older/agricultural people mid 20th century. Covers phonological, lexical, morphological and syntactical aspects in a series of maps.

PALGRAVE, F.M.T. *A List of Words and Phrases in Everyday Use by the Natives of Hetton-le-Hole in the County of Durham* (English Dialect Society vol.74, 1896, reprinted Gateshead 1997)
Useful and compassionate word-list, with pronunciation and sentence-context given for a large range of words.

PEACOCK, Robert B. *A Glossary of the dialect of
the Hundred of Consdale...in the Co of Lancaster* ed.
J C Atkinson (London, 1869)
Extensive word-list with etymological data

PEARCE, Howard *The Mark o' the Deil & other
Northumbrian Tales* (London,1894)
Short stories in dialect.

PETYT, K.M. *The Study of Dialect* (London, 1980)
Survey of the history of interest in dialect from
C18th onwards.

RAY, John *A Collection of English Words, not
generally used, with their significations and
original...* (London, 1674)
Considerable list of dialect words, grouped into
North and South, collected by Ray and friends, with
etymologies based on Skinner's *Etymologicon* and
Somner's *Saxon Dictionary*. Expanded in
subsequent editions e.g. 3rd (1737).

RITSON, Joseph *The Bishoprick Garland, or
Durham Minstrel: A choice collectin of excellent
songs relating to the above County* (Stockton, 1784,
repr. Newcastle 1792. repr. London 1810 as item 1
in 'Northern Garlands')

RITSON, Joseph (ed.) *The Northumberland Garland,
or, Newcastle Nightingale: A matchless collection of
famous songs* (Newcastle, 1793)

RITSON: *Joseph Ritson: Scholar-at-Arms* by
Bertrand H. BRONSON (Berkeley, Calif., 1938, 2
vols.)
Ch.8 deals with Ritson's work in Co.Durham.

RITSON: *Joseph Ritson: A critical biography* by
Henry A. BURD (Illinois,1916)
Study of the early dialect editor, esp. good on his
politics.

ROBINSON, Francis K. *A Glossary of Yorkshire Words and Phrases* (1855)

ROBSON, J.P. (ed.) *Songs of the Bards of the Tyne* (Newcastle ca.1849)
Collection of Tyneside songs, with glossary.

ROBSON, W.J. *The Adventures of Jackie Robison* (und.)

SHARP, Cuthbert (ed.) *A Bishoprick Garland* (1834, repr. Sunderland 1906)

SHIELDS: *The Shields Song Book, Being a collection of comic and sentimental songs, never before published, written by gentlemen of the neighbourhood* (South Shields, 1826)

SHIELDS, Mike 'Dialects of North-Eastern England', *Lore & Language* 10 (Sheffield Univ., 1974) 3-9.
Analysis of pronunciations in Newcastle and Durham areas, applying 'Geordie' strictly to speech of Newcastle, plus area up to 5 miles north and south of the lower Tyne.

SMITH, W. Herbert *Walks in Weardale* (Claypath, Durham, 1883)
General tourist guide, with walks, lists of flowers, birds, geological features etc. Gives etymologies of local words (via Skeat) pp.69-79; lists of Weardale sheep-counting numbers (pp.72-76), and list of dialect words (pp.90-96).

SOLOMON: *Dialect Songs of Solomon* (1859)
The Old Testament text translated into a range of dialects, including several versions from the North-East. including 'The Song of Solomon in the Durham Dialect as Spoken at St John's Chapel, Weardale', trans. Thomas Moore.

STAGG, John *Miscellaneous Poems, Some of which are in the Cumberland Dialect* (2nd edn, Workington, 1805)

THOMPSON, T. et al. (eds.) *A Collection of Songs...chiefly in the Newcastle Dialect* (Newcastle 1827)

TODD, George *Todd's Geordie Words and Phrases* (Newcastle 1977)
"A refresher course for lapsed Geordies."

TWEDDELL, G.M. (ed.) *Bards and Authors of Cleveland and South Durham* (Stokesley 1872)

TWEDDEL, G.M. (ed.) *Rhymes and Sketches to Illustrate the Cleveland Dialect* (Stokesley 1875)
Poems and prose, with glossary.

UMPLEBY, A.S. *A Bo'ddin o' Cowls: Verses in the Cleveland dialect* (Cambridge, 1937)

UPTON, Clive, at al. (eds) *Word Maps: A dialect atlas of England* (Beckenham, 1987)
Useful, clear presentation of dialect material similar to that in Orton's atlas.

UPTON, CLIVE, et al. (eds) *Survey of English Dialects: Dictionary and grammar* (London, 1994)
Word list, giving distribution and pronunciation, based on research in the 50s and 60s. Not assimilated in my list, but sampling shows restriction of word availability since 1900.

VIERECK, Wolfgang *Phonematische Analyse des Dialekts von Gateshead-upon-Tyne, Co. Durham* (Hamburg, 1966)
Study (in German) of one sub-dialect and its relation to standard English; includes brief and not too happy glossary on pp.97-101

VIKAR, A. *Contributions to the History of Durham Dialects* (Malmö, 1922)
Study of evidence for sound changes in medieval Durham speech via place-names etc. in charters and inventories.

WADE, Eric 'The Patter of the Northumberland and Durham Coalfield' *Bulletin of the NE Group for the Study of Labour History* 12 (1978) 21-29

WADE, Fred *The Story of South Moor: A mining village situated in the north western part of Count Durham* (typescript, 1966, held at DCL)
Immensely detailed account of local events, topography and customs, including many children's songs, adult sports, a mummers play etc. List of 'pitmatic' words, pp.187-190

WADE, Fred *The Story of West Stanley: A town in the north western part of the County of Durham; and also of Shield Row; No Place; Oxhill* (typescript,1956, held at DCL)
Includes short lives of Thomas Wilson, Alexander Barrass and Tommy Armstrong.

WADE, Fred *The Story of Tanfield and Beamish* (typscript, 1968, held at Stanley Library)
Includes texts of Bobby Shafto, Pelton Lonnin' etc.

WAKELIN, M.F. *English Dialects* (London 1972)
Readable general survey, attributing modification of N.E. dialect to immigration from Midlands (pp.105-6) and also noting immigration from Ireland, Scotland, Wales, Yorkshire, Lancashire (p.146).

WALL, Arnold 'Scandinavian Elements in the English Dialects' *Anglia* 20 (1898) 45-135

WATSON, Godfrey *Goodwife Hot and others: Northumberland's past as shown in its place names* (Alnwick, 1970)

WILSON, Joe *Tyneside Songs & Drolleries*
(Newcastle ca.1870)

WILSON, Thomas *The Pitman's Pay & other poems*
(2nd edition 1872)
Includes glossary prepared by the author, referring
back to early decades of C19th

WRIGHT, Joseph (ed.) *English Dialect Dictionary* (6
vols, Oxford, 1898-1905)
Immense survey of dialect vocabulary, drawing on
both printed sources and local research.

WRIGHT, Joseph *The English Dialect Grammar*
(Oxford, 1905)
Mostly on the phonology of dialect development;
some short notes on syntax, and an extended
glossary of the local pronunciation of standard
English words (which also in his larger Dialect
Dictionary).

WRIGHT, Thomas *Dictionary of Obsolete and
Provincial English* (2 vols, London, 1857)
Only a few references to Co.Durham, perhaps from
pre-existing printed sources.

YORKSHIRE: *The Yorkshire Dialect, Exemplified in
        various Dialogues, Tales & Songs... to which
        is added a Glossary* (London, 1839)

Other Centre for Northern Studies publications:

To Make Their Mark

David Neville

"It is a very useful addition to recent local studies which have helped to challenge received wisdoms about Edwardian England."

June Hannam. *Labour History Review*.

£7.99. Copies available from the Centre for Northern Studies.

NORTHERN REVIEW

A journal of regional and cultural affairs

"Britain's finest regional journal."
Ian Jack.

Back issues available from the Centre for Northern Studies,
at £8.00 each.

NORTH EAST HISTORY

NORTH EAST HISTORY

Volume 31 1997

NORTH EAST HISTORY

Volume 32 1998

A refereed Journal that covers the region during the modern period.

**For subscription details and back issues please contact the
Centre for Northern Studies.**